GASLIGHTING

How to Classify, Counter, and Conquer the Covert Control of Others

PRISCILLA POSEY

© Copyright 2019 by Priscilla Posey - All rights reserved.

The content contained within this book may not be reproduced, duplicated or transmitted without direct written permission from the author or the publisher.

Under no circumstances will any blame or legal responsibility be held against the publisher, or author, for any damages, reparation, or monetary loss due to the information contained within this book. Either directly or indirectly.

Legal Notice:

This book is copyright protected. This book is only for personal use. You cannot amend, distribute, sell, use, quote or paraphrase any part, or the content within this book, without the consent of the author or publisher.

Disclaimer Notice:

Please note the information contained within this document is for educational and entertainment purposes only. All effort has been executed to present accurate, up to date, and reliable, complete information. No warranties of any kind are declared or implied. Readers acknowledge that the author is not engaging in the rendering of legal, financial, medical or professional advice. The content within this book has been derived from various sources. Please consult a licensed professional before attempting any techniques outlined in this book.

By reading this document, the reader agrees that under no circumstances is the author responsible for any losses, direct or indirect, which are incurred as a result of the use of the information contained within this document, including, but not limited to, — errors, omissions, or inaccuracies.

Table of Contents

Introduction vii

Chapter 1: Understanding the Ins and Outs of Gaslighting . 1

    History of Gaslighting 5

    Why Does Gaslighting Happen? 6

    Where Does Gaslighting Happen? 8

    Where is Gaslighting Typically Seen? 9

    Common Gaslighting Situations 11

    Emotional Hot Spots that are targeted 15

Chapter 2: Illusion vs. Reality 19

    Red Flags or Telltale Signs of Gaslighting 20

    Manipulation Techniques Used by Gaslighters 31

    Manipulative Techniques Resembling Attention -Seeking Behaviors 38

    The Key Elements of Gaslighting Success 42

Differences between Manipulation and Bad Behavior 44

Chapter 3: Manipulation Where it is Least Expected 47

Gaslighting in Families..48

Gaslighting by Adult Children.....................................53

Gaslighting in Relationships 56

Gaslighting at the Workplace.....................................58

Gaslighting in Public Life and Politics 60

Chapter 4: They're Not All the Same 65

The Manipulator Who Uses Guilt...............................66

The Aggressive Manipulator or 'Threatener' 68

The Manipulator Who Uses the Silent Treatment 70

The Manipulator Who Attacks Your Self-Esteem.................72

The Manipulator Who Uses Competition 74

The Manipulator Who Uses Criticism.......................77

The Manipulator Who Uses Charm 80

Chapter 5: Victim vs. Manipulator 83

Effects of Manipulation on the Victims....................84

Effects of Manipulation on the Manipulator...........89

What Goes On In the Minds of Manipulators? 93

Goals of Manipulation 97

Failures Commonly Encountered by Manipulators..............99

Manipulators Can Change 100

Chapter 6: Standing Up For Yourself 103

Common Tips to Help Counter Manipulation 104

    Manipulation Countering Techniques in Relationships 114

    Manipulation Countering Techniques at the Workplace ... 118

    Manipulation Countering Techniques in the Family 126

    Manipulation Countering Techniques When Dealing with Adult Children 128

Chapter 7: Path to Recovery 133

    How to Spot Manipulative Behavior and Stay Safe in the Future 134

    How to Trust Yourself Again 141

    How to Prevent Yourself from Becoming Bitter and Begin the Healing Process 144

    When to Seek Professional Help and Other Useful Resources 151

Conclusion 155

Resources 161

INTRODUCTION

"Remember, a fact is a fact, no matter how hard the liars amongst you might try hushing it up." - Billy Childish

The first thing to know about gaslighting is that you, as a victim, feel stifled and used. It is a powerfully dangerous form of emotional abuse where you are made to feel worthless and believe that the world is likely to be a better place without you. As a victim, you think that you are a useless person in any kind of relationship. Unfortunately, these imagined feelings are a result of someone else who has such immeasurable control over your life that you don't even realize it.

You are so blind to the manipulation that is happening in your life that you don't believe, not even for a second, that you are a victim. You are so caught up in pleasing and keeping the 'manipulator' happy that you forget that your life is not yours anymore. And yet, there is a deep sense of yearning to be free. Here are some classic signs of being under the control of a manipulator in your life:

- You feel that you are giving your best, and yet, you are not happy at all.

- You are confused about the relationship in question. For example, you think you have a good husband, and yet you cannot find happiness in the marriage.

- You feel you cannot work any better than this, and still, you don't stop trying to do better.

- You have problems making decisions, even the simplest ones, and are continually second-guessing yourself.

- You have absolutely no time and energy to invest in yourself.

- You don't care how you look, talk, or behave with other people except when the manipulator comments on these aspects of your personality.

- You don't care what others are saying about you. You only worry about what the manipulator is thinking of you and your behavior.

- You keep making excuses for the other person's mistakes.

- You start talking with the concerned individual, but end up feeling like you wished you hadn't started the conversation at all.

- You are obsessively worried about one or two flaws in your personality and character so much so that you begin to believe that they will become your nemesis.

- You yearn to break free but cannot find the courage and strength to do so.

And how do I know all this? Because I lived like this for many, many years before enlightenment struck me and I found the power to break free from such a pitiable existence to live my life fully and meaningfully. Here is my story.

My first encounter with a narcissist started when I was 19 years old, and lasted a seemingly interminable decade. In the days of my youth, thanks to the raging hormones and his stylish charm and wit, I fell hook, line, and sinker for this absolutely handsome man who went on to become my husband even as he worked extremely hard to make my life one living hell.

And mind you, for a very long time, I did not even realize that something was wrong with my charmer of a husband. I kept telling myself that something was wrong with me, and he was right in expecting the impossible from me. I'm sorry I've gone ahead in time. Allow me to complete my story from the very beginning.

I met him at a college party, and his electrifying smile was enough to light up the entire room. When I first looked into his captivating eyes, there seemed to be an instant connection between us. Despite being a crowded party scene, the two of us spent the entire night by ourselves and away from all the other people.

We talked the whole night and exchanged a lot of personal information. I told him why I joined a college far away from my home. It was to put as much distance as I could between me and my overbearing parents. As we spoke, we found many common likes and dislikes like, for example, we both realized that we loved the tacos sold from an almost neglected stand just off of the college campus. Very few students found the time to walk that distance for a taco!

We also spoke at length about my dreams and desires, and it looked like we had set off a lifelong friendship. He also spoke about his life until then, and his dreams and desires. The attraction between us was so strong that within two weeks of our first meeting, we were dating exclusively, and within just four months, he proposed marriage, which I accepted delightedly thinking that an idyllic life was all set for me with this wonderful man in my life. We got married very soon, and within a couple of months, I was pregnant too.

Things took a nasty turn after our marriage. My newly-acquired husband didn't need to put on any pretense of niceties (though I understood this much later in life). He started finding fault with everything I did or wanted to do.

If I didn't score 100%, he told me I was worthless and that there was no need to waste tuition money for college. Unilaterally, he pulled me out of college telling me that I should be a stay-at-home parent for the family. At that time, it made sense to me, and I thought his expectations were reasonable.

However, things got slowly but steadily out of hand. If he didn't like the dinner I prepared, he would empty his plate into the garbage and order pizza for himself. On the other hand, even if, on rare occasions, he cooked and burned the dish, I was not allowed to eat the burned food without complaining. He would become uncontrollably livid if I made any attempt to point out his mistakes.

If his clothes were not ironed well enough to meet his stringent expectations, he would not hesitate to command me to wake up in the morning to correct these 'mistakes.' This unpleasant attitude was displayed even at the cost of waking up our baby daughter at an unearthly hour.

All my protests were drowned in the unilateral argument that it was my job to look after him and do everything in my power to meet his needs and requirements. I was expected to be perfect in everything I did; care for him and our daughter and get perfect scores. That he didn't have to do these things was an accepted law between us, which I also took with little or no protest of any kind. It was amazing how he was able to make it look like everything was happening naturally and correctly.

I truly believed that I was not worthy of going to college, and my only job was to take care of his needs, and to do that perfectly. I convinced myself that, after all, he was going to work to provide for us, and it was my duty to take care of our home, our daughter, and my husband's needs to perfection.

At that point in time, it made sense to me that this was his way of displaying his love for me. He wanted me to be a cut above the rest and achieve higher standards than the average.

Over time, things got worse. His criticisms were direct and hurtful. For example, he would call me fat if I ate something against his wishes. He would command me to change my dress if he believed that it had a low-cut neck more than necessary. He would tell me to adjust or even remove my makeup if he thought it was excessive! If I protested or fought against these mean attitudes, he would accuse me of cheating on him.

And eventually, my life reached such abysmal limits that I could do nothing without getting my husband's (thankfully, ex now) approval or consent. Suddenly one day, I woke up to the realization that I couldn't do this anymore, and once this idea hit me, I felt a sense of liberation, and consequently, I found the courage to open up about my feelings and life experiences to my friends.

After listening to my anecdotes and experiences, one friend told me to read up and learn about narcissism. I was amazed at the number of attitudinal references to the narcissism that I could easily identify in my husband's behavior. The deeper I delved into the subject of narcissistic personality disorder, the greater was my realization of my husband's personality problems, and the more I realized how I had been living the life of a completely ignorant fool blaming myself for all the problems of my life. I was completely under the control of a manipulative and controlling person without realizing that he had a personality disorder, and I was at the receiving end of it.

And with this realization came the power to slowly but steadily disentangle myself from the claws of my husband until he became my ex and I was completely free of his influence over my life. The only way out for me was to get out of the highly toxic relationship.

However, for some of you, this 'finality' need not be the case. Fortunately, some of you could be in a place from which you could salvage and repair things and set right all concerned stakeholders, including the person with the manipulative personality disorder.

This book is written with the intention of passing on my learning and the little wisdom I gained through my experiences and consultations with experts in the field to people in need of this kind of advice. This book is my comprehensive guide to what narcissistic minds are, how to best engage a narcissist, how to interact with others in regard to supporting you in your journey, and some bonus chapters that I found might provide some useful content. Hopefully, you will find this book useful as you begin your journey to understanding the narcissistic mind, and you will find valuable insight into why narcissists do what they do. Read on, and I sincerely hope this book will help you break your leash and find freedom and happiness, slowly but surely.

As A Token
of My Gratitude...

I'd like to offer you this amazing resource which my clients pay for. It is a report I written when I first began my journey.

Click on the picture above or navigate to the website below to join my exclusive email list. Upon joining, you will receive this incredible report on how to recognize an abusive relationship.

If you ask most people on the street what an abusive relationship is, chances are you'd get a description of physical abuse. And yes, that is most certainly an abusive relationship. However, abuse comes in many forms. The actual meaning of abuse is when someone exerts control over another person.

Find out more about recognizing an abusive relationship and learn how to take control over your life by clicking on the book above or by going to this link:

https://tinyurl.com/RecognizeAbusiveRelationship

CHAPTER 1

Understanding the Ins and Outs of Gaslighting

In 1944, a movie called *Gaslight* was released that changed the way people thought about manipulation and its immense power. This movie shows the story of a husband character that manipulates his wife and her life to such an extent that she begins to believe that she has become insane.

In this movie too, just like in my life, the wife, Paula, gets completely caught up with the charms of Gregory, the man who woos and wins her. After a whirlwind romance, they get married, and then the tragedy begins. Gregory begins to show his true personality so subtly that Paula begins to think that everything is alright with her husband and that she is going crazy.

The husband in the film dimmed the gas lights in the house and insisted that the wife imagined that the light was dim. His insistence and manipulation were so powerful that the poor, hapless woman begins to think that she is going crazy. And so, the name gaslighting came to be used for such devious and evil manipulative tactics to deliberately steer people away from their real lives and life experiences.

The movie itself is based on a 1938 play of the same name. The ultimate aim of the villainous husband was, of course, to drive his wife to insanity so that he could put her away in a mental institution and claim her inheritance.

Gaslighting is the name used by psychologists to refer to the tactics used by people with a personality disorder to control and manipulate the lives of other people, either individuals or a group of people. These tactics are so strong and go so deep that the manipulated people tend to doubt and question everything in their own lives; their reality, perceptions, feelings, experiences, and interpretations of these experiences. If someone can have this kind of maniacal control over your life, then there is little doubt that your life and sanity are in danger.

At this juncture, it is important to differentiate gaslighting from those tactics that many people use to annoy and irritate the people around them. Gaslighting tactics have a dark quality that annoying but innocuous behavior of certain people doesn't have. It is imperative that you clearly differentiate between the two so that you don't end up judging everyone you come across wrongly.

But you must know for certain that gaslighting is a very serious problem, and you must learn to discern such behavior and stay as far away from such people as possible. After all, having your reality taken from you can be quite dangerous, and if not managed sensibly can prove disastrous for you and your loved ones.

The difficult thing about understanding gaslighting is that the behavioral signs might start out as something very small and insignificant. For example, the manipulator could correct a small detail in a story or life experience you are narrating. Of course, then his or her correction makes sense, and you accept it wholeheartedly. Slowly, that 'past victory' becomes the focal point and keeps rearing its ugly head in all your interactions with the concerned individual, and before you know it, you become his or her slave completely losing touch with your reality and life.

Deliberately, you will be pushed to such an extent that taking simple daily decisions might become difficult for you. Driven by the seeds of self-doubt sowed by the gaslighter, you could find yourself second-guessing every decision you make. Like I already told you in the introduction chapter, even the clothes I wore became my husband's decision. At some point, the victim is likely to feel that he or she cannot take any decision whatsoever and depends on every little thing on the manipulator.

Furthermore, the aggressor will slowly convince you that his or her behavior is also your fault. The more you apologize for your behavior, the greedier the aggressor's ego becomes, and the person demands an increasing level of apology and supplicating behavior from you.

The aggressor gets so deep into his or her gaslighting attitude that you will find it exceedingly difficult to reach out and seek help from other people in the fear that they will go against your aggressor. When you are completely and irrevocably under the aggressor's control, then the person dumps you and seeks new 'conquests.'

History of Gaslighting

While the term 'gaslighting' was introduced during the early 1940s, the concept of manipulative behavior for controlling people and altering people's imagined realties has been part of human history for a long time. The victims were simply 'diagnosed' with this condition. They simply withered away in a lunatic asylum or some other institution, alone, depressed, and completely neglected.

Can you recall the story of 'The Emperor Clothes?' What happened there? Did the smart salesman drive every observer on the street to believe that the emperor was clothed in the finest of garments when, in reality, he was stark naked? A little, guileless child saved the day for the rest of the people who believed that if they couldn't see the clothes on their emperor, then it was their fault.

In 1981, psychologist Edward Weinshel wrote an article entitled "Some Clinical Consequences of Introjection: Gaslighting," in which he explained the concept in the following way. The manipulator 'externalizes and projects' the image or thought, and the victim 'internalizes and assimilates' the information into his or her psyche unquestioningly. The 'victim' takes in all the faults, mistakes, and irrationality in such relationships.

Why Does Gaslighting Happen?
Simply put, gaslighting is all about having control. This need for control or domination could stem from personality disorders like narcissism, antisocial issues, unresolved childhood trauma, or any other reason.

Gaslighting behavior is usually seen between people involved in power dynamics where one person invariably wields more power than the other person or people in the relationship equation. The victim of gaslighting tactics is typically on a lower rung than the manipulator and is also terrified of losing something in the relationship. The target of the manipulative relationship is likely to be a codependent partner in the relationship.

For example, in a romantic relationship, the wife might feel the compulsion to put up with manipulative behavior because she WANTS to be in the relationship and/or desires the other things that it brings. Such people are ready to change their perceptions to align with those of the manipulative partner so as to avoid conflicts and to allow things to happen smoothly.

Understanding the Ins and Outs of Gaslighting

On the other hand, the manipulator continues to be one because he or she is scared of being seen as something less important or significant than desired. Another critical perspective of the gaslighter is that the person may not realize that he or she is behaving in ways that could harm or hurt the 'target.' They could be indulging in gaslighting tactics simply because they were reared like that.

For example, if a person was brought up by parents who believe in the concept of absolute certainty, then this person may not know that other perspectives can exist and that they can be right. Such people could be primed to think that anyone who has a different approach or perspective is wrong. Further, they could believe that people with these 'wrong' notions should be corrected, and thus resort to gaslighting tactics; an approach found commonly in a family and among loved ones.

And then, there are the ones who employ gaslighting to show off their dominance and power with little or no care toward the pain and agony inflicted on the target. Sometimes, the 'dominance and power' could also be a facade for the manipulator's insecurities and fears. Whatever it is, gaslighting is employed to dominate unfairly over other people.

Where Does Gaslighting Happen?

Gaslighting can happen and be experienced by anyone and everyone. For example, you could be a victim of such tactics from your spouse, partner, colleague, or sometimes, even a parent. In fact, gaslighting tactics are not restricted to the personal or professional realm.

Gaslighting strategies are used even in public life, affecting an entire group of people. There are multiple instances in which you can clearly see gaslighting techniques by President Donald Trump and his administration. Most experts agree that politics is a field where spreading lies is taken and accepted to be a stereotypical attitude. However, President Trump seems to have taken it a bit too far.

In the initial days of his office, President Trump - along with his administration staff - are believed to have lied so blatantly that there was a shade of arrogance and utter contempt for the intelligence of the American people. It was like the concerned officials were baiting the common people, telling them to rise up and revolt against the nastiness if you can; this was a clear sign of narcissistic personality disorder.

For instance, the administration lied about the crowd size at the Presidential swearing-in. It was clear that photos from President Obama's swearing-in were manipulated to look like the current one. It was so easy to detect this lie that for some people, it was like a war cry to the media, which was most likely to be discredited by Americans for putting such lies on their websites and publications.

At a personal level, gaslighting tactics are used by manipulative people who want to control the lives of their family members. Think of a physically and emotionally abusive spouse wreaking havoc on his or her partner or the children in the family, and you can easily discern gaslighting behavior.

Where is Gaslighting Typically Seen?

Geographically speaking, gaslighting behavior is not exclusive to any part of the world. Wherever power dynamics are in play and where the need and desire for control over people and resources exist, gaslighting behavior can be witnessed. Multiple studies reveal that this kind of unpleasant and dangerous behavior is prevalent not only in personal relationships but also at the workplace, and even in public life as in the way some politicians and their coterie interact with the common man on the street.

Gaslighting

MHR, an HR services provider, conducted a survey in the UK which revealed some shocking numbers. Over 3000 people undertook the survey, and 58% of this group claimed that they had experienced what they believed was gas-lighting behavior at their workplace. About 30% said they did not experience such behavior while 12% said that they didn't know! The disturbing results of this survey poll reveal how widespread gaslighting is in the UK. Some examples of gaslighting behaviors at the workplace include:

- Taking credit for your work
- Mocking you, your behavior or dress style in front of other colleagues
- Setting unreasonable and unrealistic deadlines
- Deliberately withholding information that is crucial for the success of a project you are working on

Most of the elements mentioned above are seemingly insignificant but add up to a lot in retrospect. And moreover, unlike bullying, which is easily discernible, gaslighting behaviors are subtle and are meant to slowly but surely put doubt on your capabilities and value to the organization. Such attitudes cannot be caught until after the damage is done to the target's psyche.

Another US-based report says that 3 out of 4 people in the country are not aware of the term, and this state of ignorance is despite the widespread prevalence of gaslighting behavior in the entertainment and media industries where power-play dynamics are perhaps the strongest.

Nearly 75% of the surveyed people said that they had heard of the term but did not know its meaning. The study revealed that about a third of the female population had termed their romantic partners as 'crazy' or 'insane' in a very serious way. About 25% of the male population had also used these two words to describe their partners.

Therefore, gaslighting behavior is not restricted to any particular geography or industry, and can be witnessed in different countries, cultures, and industries.

Common Gaslighting Situations

Here are some common examples of gaslighting scenarios that could help you understand if and when you are being gaslighted by various perpetrators.

Gaslighting

In a home environment - Alice's father, Andrew, is a bitter and angry man who is carrying a lot of negativity right from his childhood. His power play is most evident with Alice, thanks to her dependence on him for a lot of things. Alice's mother is the breadwinner in the family and is away most of the time at work.

Alice spent a lot more time with her father than her mother and had unwittingly built herself into a codependency situation with Andrew. She was highly sensitive to his mood swings and was always worried that some action or behavior of hers would bring on a dark mood in her father.

Whenever her father was in a dark mood, he would lash out at Alice by saying that 'You're worthless,' 'I wonder why you were born,' and quite frequently using foul language too. If Alice tried to argue back with him, he would laugh it off and say, 'Why are you so unnecessarily sensitive?'

Alice had become so accustomed to this situation at home that she did not even think it important enough to speak to her mother about it that was too busy with her work to find time for her daughter. Alice was completely under her father's control and even accepted it as natural. She believed that her father was only helping her toward self-improvement and that there was nothing wrong with him.

Another common situation is when adult children manipulate their old parents. Here is a sample case that you are likely to find in many homes. This topic is discussed in detail in the subsequent chapter.

In a romantic relationship - In the eyes of most people, Julie's life could be seen as being as ideal. Married for over five years to her first love who is now an adoring husband, financially secure (her husband, John, is an investment banker who rakes in the moolah), and with two beautiful children, Julie might look like there is no dearth of happiness in her life. And yet, she knows what she is going through. Before her marriage, Julie was an artist with some great skills.

After she got married, John did his best to prevent his wife from trying to advance her skills and make a name for herself in the art world. He always found fault with her work and made her feel worthless. Every time she tried to paint something, he would say, 'A lousy artist like you is not going to make it in the art world which is filled with brilliant artists. Your work will never match up to theirs.

Gaslighting

Don't waste time and money on this. Instead, just focus on looking after the family.'

Also, he would always bring up a bad experience that she had had during her early artist days. She had created a painting and wanted feedback from a famous artist who was a good friend of her husband's. The man had said that her skills were way below even an average artist and that she should not even try moving forward. Julie's husband never failed to bring up that comment and used it to make her believe that she was fit for nothing more than taking care of the family.

Julie's husband used that one bad experience and feedback to remind her of her worthlessness continually, and repeated practice and such habitual behavior enslaved her to her husband completely. Now, although she lives comfortably, she realizes that her life is actually empty. She wants to break free from her husband's manipulative ways, but he uses their children to strengthen his power over her.

In a workplace scenario - Jolly was a salesgirl in a large cosmetic showroom. After working for five years, she was given a promotion to work in another section, which not only gave her a higher salary but also opened up career growth prospects. Jolly was very happy with the promotion and started working with her new boss, Penny.

Initially, Jolly found Penny helpful and sweet. Slowly, Penny started passing on insignificant tasks to Jolly, who did them uncomplainingly. However, this did not stop at all and, in fact, increased so much that she had no time and energy to learn anything new at the job. She was just about able to finish all the work assigned by her boss, who kept her at arm's length and discouraged interactions of all kinds except with giving out tasks.

A department meeting was called one day, and Jolly was part of it. Penny addressed the other people and said, 'Meet Jolly, who has been with us for nearly three months now, and she has yet to learn the ropes of the new department. I hope she catches up soon or else we might have to send her back after demoting her.' Jolly turned red with embarrassment and shame at this open and unexpected insult from her boss. And she realized that she had unwittingly become a victim of gaslighting tactics!

Emotional Hot Spots that are targeted

Nearly anyone can be a target to gaslighting tactics considering the subtlety involved in the process. Very few people can really discern the difference between gaslighting and simple annoying behavior. Most often, people will tend to categorize gaslighting behaviors as a mere annoyance and tend to ignore it. Yet, there are certain types of people who become easy targets for gaslighting. Some of them are:

Empaths - Empaths are people who are extremely sensitive to everything that is happening around them. They can quickly, and most often, unwittingly absorb both positive and negative energies from their environment. Such people can be easy targets for gaslighters because it is quite easy to influence them. Just sending negative vibes to empaths can enhance their sensitivity to a gaslighter's needs.

Insecure people - Gaslighters typically target people with significant inferiority complexes. Men and women who feel insecure about themselves are easy targets considering that they are already in a vulnerable condition.

Moreover, insecure people are continuously looking for positive affirmation from others, which is exactly what gaslighters want in the initial stages of any new relationship. Gaslighting tactics start with heaping praise, often when it is not necessary and praises on the victims initially, and once they are trapped, the true color of gaslighters come to the fore.

And yet, it is time to reiterate that some gaslighters are so good at what they do that even the sanest and most sensible people can become their targets. Therefore, it makes sense to be aware of the concept of gaslighting tactics and their multiple negative effects and to be wary of such people.

Gaslighting

CHAPTER 2

Illusion vs. Reality

So, now that you know the definition, history, and other basic aspects of gaslighting, we can go on to red flags that should help you understand whether you are a victim of gaslighting tactics. In addition to being aware of red flags, you must be able to identify different kinds of techniques used in gas-lighting tactics. This kind of knowledge will build your self-awareness and also guide you on how to handle such elements before they get out of hand.

It is imperative that you recognize the signs of gaslighting tactics as quickly as you can. Such situations if left unresolved can result in anxiety and depression, which, in turn, can lead to irrevocable, sometimes even fatal, outcomes. Victims are frequently known to have nervous breakdowns.

So, read on and be on your guard to ensure you lead a life free from being unduly victimized simply due to your naiveté. Build your mental and emotional strength with the power of knowledge.

Red Flags or Telltale Signs of Gaslighting

You 'feel' or 'sense that something is 'off' - It could be anyone; your partner, spouse, parent, sibling, friend, boss, or anybody else. You cannot place your finger on the core issue. But, you 'sense' that something is wrong about this person. If you keep thinking like this about a person, then it is definitely a tell-tale sign. Sometimes, it might be someone else you trust who can feel this way about the person you are getting eerily close to.

Here is an example to illustrate this. I had already told you that I met my ex-husband when I was just 19, and I was floored by his personality and behavior. I raved about him to my best friend, Betty, who, by the way, did not attend the party when I met him for the first time.

I was insistent that he meet my best friend as soon as possible. In fact, I had told him that I would bring her to meet him at our next date. He said okay then. But, he canceled our next date giving some weird excuse. Even though I felt uneasy, I left it like that.

When we were fixing up our date again, the first question was about Betty. He wanted to know if she would come. Coincidentally, she was busy and could not have come to meet him. He readily agreed to come for the next date. We met, and again, I came away completely swept off my feet. Now I look back, and I realize that he worked very hard to make sure that he did not meet Betty for nearly three months. Betty found his behavior strange and kept warning me about him saying that something was definitely off. I brushed it off, saying she was reading too much into a trivial thing.

Then, one fine day, Betty just turned up at one of our dates giving some feeble excuse that she was in the area, and wanted to drop in and say hello to my boyfriend. Incidentally, even I was unaware of her sudden appearance. But, my partner was livid and made it seem that I had deliberately set a trap for him to meet Betty. He didn't speak to me for nearly a week blaming me for the incident. I had to literally beg him to forgive me for doing something he did not like. You see, I had almost become the slave of his charm and good looks by then.

I have to give it to Betty for being honest with me and telling me to my face that she picked up negative vibes from my boyfriend and warned me about him. It was my error of judgment (I thought she was just jealous) that prevented me from heeding her warning.

Now when I look back, I realize that if a simple routine event of meeting my best friend could trigger an unreasonable reaction from my husband, shouldn't I have accepted that something was really 'off?'

You feel threatened by the concerned person, but you don't know why - Tom is your father, and you want to do things that make him happy. But, you also feel a deep sense of threat in his presence. He is smiling at you, and yet, you feel fearful. You don't know why. This seemingly inexplicable feeling is rooted in your instincts. However, you are not ready to heed your gut feelings because you are scared of losing the one man who seems to love you.

Illusion vs. Reality

Here is another example of this kind of threatening to feel you could have experienced. Your husband appears to care for and love you. You can see him walking toward you with an affectionate smile on his face. But you flinch instinctively because you 'sense' he is going to hurt you. But you don't have any obvious or tangible reason to 'feel' like this.

You are frequently second-guessing your memory - One of the first things that gaslighting tactics target is your memory. Manipulators invariably start by doubting what you are saying. Look at the following conversation:

Victim - I must tell you about how I won an award for acting in my freshman year. I played the role of Lady Macbeth, and everyone raved about my acting skills. It's a memory I cherish, you know.

Manipulator - Really? I thought you told me you had stage fright and didn't particularly care for performing on stage? Remember that time in your school days that you told me about when you were so scared that you couldn't say a word and had to walk off the stage when the audience began to boo? You told me how embarrassed you felt about the entire incident.

Gaslighting

Manipulator (continues, even as the victim is trying to recall this incident) - Are you sure you won the award because you were good or because there was no one else vying for the prize?

The victim feels flummoxed and tries to recall every minute detail of that event which is likely to make her or him unsure of what actually happened. Such manipulative and doubt-creating experiences are repeated frequently by the manipulator, and very soon, the victim begins to second-guess every memory from past life.

You feel disoriented and confused - You remember keeping the car keys in the bowl near the door when you returned from work yesterday. Now, you can't find them there, and your husband looks for them and finds the keys in the freezer! He tells you that this is not the first time you have put the keys there.

You are asking yourself if you really put the keys in the freezer. You can't believe you could do such a thing. Yet, the keys were there in the freezer. A few minutes ago you could vividly recall the scene where you remember dropping the keys in the designated bowl. But, now with the keys in the freezer, you cannot recall that memory anymore. You are confused and disoriented about your life.

You are always focusing on your character flaws - The primary purpose of a gaslighter is to make you feel less worthy of yourself, which is achieved by relentlessly focusing and reminding you of your faults. Continuous interactions with such people are likely to have made you focus excessively on your flaws rather than your strengths. Your self-esteem is likely to be at abysmally low levels.

So, if you find yourself always looking for your faults in any given situation, then it could be an important gaslighting tell-tale sign. For example, if you have had a fight with your partner and if you look back at the scene with the intention of how you could have done something differently to prevent the fight without thinking of your partner's mistakes, then it's time to wake up to reality. Again, retrospective thought in this way occasionally is fine. But, if you are doing at every instance, then it could be a cause for concern.

You always feel you should apologize - You are a good worker in the office, and your earlier bosses had always praised you for your dedication and hard work. However,

Gaslighting

with your new boss, Ben, you feel inadequate about your capabilities. He keeps finding fault with your work, and most often, you feel he is right. You feel compelled to keep apologizing to Ben for your mistakes.

You have completed a complex and multilayered report by Sunday evening working extremely hard right through the weekend. You send the report late Sunday night by mail to Ben. He responds almost immediately with a spelling error you made on the body of the email. You spelled report 'reprot.' Ben did not even open the attached report. Instead, he chose to find one little fault that hardly mattered.

Ordinarily, people would have lashed out at Ben for this email and would have reminded him that they had been working the entire weekend and he has the nerve to come back with a small spelling error! However, you feel the need to say sorry in such a situation! This is a sure sign of being a victim of gaslighting tactics.

Furthermore, when you apologized for the error, Ben's reply was to tell you not to overreact. He only pointed out an obvious mistake, he said. You again feel the need to apologize for overreacting. These conflicting emotions drive you nuts, and you don't know what to do.

You always feel you are not 'good enough' - Gaslighting victims are not restricted by gender. Both men and women can be caught in the web of deceit and lies. For example, I knew of a lady who was not just beautiful but also very talented. She could paint, draw, sing, and dance. She was the breadwinner in the family while her husband looked after the home.

In this kind of power dynamic, the lady friend, Brenda, used gaslighting tactics to control her husband. She kept reminding him of his 'average' money-earning capabilities. She never failed to tell him that if it was not for her ability to rake in the moolah, the family would have reeled in poverty.

The poor man was continually made to feel that he was not good enough for his wife. He always felt disappointed in himself and his capabilities. Consequently, he felt compelled to accept the humiliation and insult that Brenda wrought on him uncomplainingly. He felt that this was his way of contributing to the relationship.

If he had only stopped to think, he would have realized that she needed him more than he needed her. He was a qualified accountant and could have easily made a reasonably good amount of money for his family's sustenance. However, Brenda needed her husband to 'add' to her capabilities. Thanks to her seemingly happy family, the world thought that she was not only beautiful and talented but also ran a wonderful home!

You think you are going crazy - This feeling is not a simple 'going mad on a hectic day' kind of experience. When you are a victim of gaslighting tactics, you feel neurotic and begin to believe that something is wrong with your head and that you need help. Sometimes, this neurotic feeling is so deeply ensconced in your mind that you may think that nothing can help you anymore, and the only way out is 'going out,' which leads to suicidal tendencies.

'Feeling neurotic' is as close to the final target that the gaslighter wants you to reach. He or she is working slowly but surely towards making you feel that you cannot live without them. You find yourself unable to understand what is happening around you and that you need the gaslighter to interpret and spoon-feed you. You think you will die if he or she is not around you at all times.

You feel alone and hopeless - This is usually the final act of submission. You feel so alone and hopeless that your life seems empty. You begin to live like an automaton and don't find the power to connect with anyone, even those who truly care for and love you.

In fact, you feel so alone and hopeless that you believe that you are not worthy of love. So, if someone approaches you affectionately or even in a friendly manner, you either withdraw completely or lash out at them because these reactions become your surviving techniques. You choose to blank out all forms of emotion, hoping you feel less pain than before.

For example, as a wife, you could be the victim of gas-lighting tactics and be under the control of your manipulative husband. However, your parents and siblings truly care for you, and they realize that something is wrong in your life and want to help you. But, your sense of loneliness is so deep that you keep them out of your life and counter their moves to get close to you. Irrationally, you continue to hang on to your manipulative husband, thinking he is the only one who can remove the feeling of loneliness and hopelessness in your life.

Other tell-tale signs that should alert you to impending dangers of being a gaslighting victim are:

- You feel scared all the time and don't trust yourself to take the correct decision.

Gaslighting

- You are scared of something but cannot pinpoint the cause of your fear.

- You tense up physically and mentally whenever the gaslighter is close by.

- You recall happy moments in your past life with sadness.

- You think you are not the same person you were in the past.

- You think your life has changed drastically. But, you are uncertain of what exactly has changed.

- Interestingly, you are also addicted to the grandiose attitude of your manipulator so much so that you need those brief moments of love and affection (even if it is fake) from him or her to be happy.

- You remember yourself to have been a bubbly, happy person who never thought twice about expressing opinions. However, nowadays, you feel scared of saying what you want to say and choose to remain silent most of the time.

Therefore, if you are experiencing any of the feelings mentioned above, don't believe you are going crazy. You could be the victim of gaslighting tactics. Think as objectively as you can and examine your life and your surroundings.

Manipulation Techniques Used by Gaslighters

So, how do manipulators manage to control people? Are there specific techniques they use? Yes, these techniques can be labeled and are easily discernible. Manipulators learn by experience and know which technique is the optimal choice in any given situation. Here are some of the techniques that manipulators employ for gaslighting:

Withholding - Gaslighters use the 'withholding' technique to hold back certain elements, including critical information in the relationship. Here are some examples:

- A husband refusing to acknowledge or pretending not to see the pain that his wife is going through is withholding an element that is essential to keep the relationship healthy.

- A mother who refuses to share her emotions with her teenage daughter is also holding back something that could help the latter cope with the struggles of adolescence.

- A boss pretending not to understand what his subordinate is telling him is a withholding tactic.

- A boss holding back important data that prevents the victim from achieving optimal results

- A partner who refuses to accept that he can help around the house is also employing withholding tactics.

One of the most significant consequences of the withholding tactic is to prevent people from getting a chance of a fair solution to problems and issues.

Blocking/Diverting - The abuser controls any given situation through the use of blocking or diverting. For example, an abusive parent could say things like, 'I'm not having this conversation tonight. We've spent a lot of time and energy on it already.' The parent closes the discussion by saying there's nothing more to discuss.

Trivializing - Also referred to as minimizing, this technique is used by gaslighters to trivialize your feelings and thoughts. For example, if you went to your boss and said, "I was hurt by your words," then a manipulator's typical reply would be, 'Why are you making such a big fuss about it?' Or 'Why are you so sensitive over something so trivial?' or 'I was only kidding. Why are you taking it so seriously?'

Not only do such replies enhance your feelings of hurt, but they could also make you feel quite stupid, increasing your sense of self-doubt. When the abuser repeatedly trivializes your feelings and thoughts, you begin to feel that you are overreacting, and soon, cease to talk about your feelings or opinions openly.

Forgetting or Being in Denial - Manipulators use the denial tactic by refusing to acknowledge your thoughts and feelings. They avoid your side of the story altogether either by conveniently forgetting or simply denying things that you might have spoken about earlier. In fact, denial tactics are used particularly in those instances in which the victim wants closure. Look at the following conversation between a husband and wife where the husband is the abuser.

Husband - What rubbish! You never said that you have a party to attend this weekend. You must have dreamed the conversation you had with me.

Wife - But, I did. I told you about it when we were having dinner on Wednesday.

Gaslighting

Husband - Now, I've proof that you are dreaming up or lying about the conversation. I was traveling on Wednesday and did not return until midnight. How could we have had dinner that day?

Now, the wife is confused. Did she or did she not tell her husband about the party? When did she have dinner with him? Was it not Thursday? The seeds of self-doubt have been planted in her mind by her manipulative husband using the denial tactic.

Changing the subject - Another gaslighting technique commonly used by manipulators is to change the subject if you raise a subject they don't want to discuss. For example, if you were to ask him about a promise that he made to take you shopping today, he would turn around and ask you a completely different question like, 'Did you talk to your mother about babysitting our child while we attend the office party tonight?'

This sudden change of subject is likely to take your thoughts away from what you were asking him. And what's more, you could have genuinely forgotten to ask your mother. Now, the scene is set for him to attack you for your forgetfulness and reiterate his point that something is happening to you. Your self-doubt could take a big leap forward.

Twisting and reframing - Experienced manipulators are great at using this technique. They are skilled at taking a statement you made during an earlier conversation and twisting and reframing it to suit their needs and to their advantage. Abusers efficiently pick out sentences and place them out of context resulting in multiple consequences, including:

- You begin to second-guess yourself more often than before

- Your words would be twisted in such a way that you could be made out to be a villain, or worse still, crazy

For example, if you accused your abusive partner of hitting your son and confronted him, he could come up with something like this, 'I didn't hit your son. I only smacked him lightly at the back of his head. And anyway, it's good that someone was responsible enough to correct his behavior.'

Also, abusers use this technique to discredit you among your friends and loved ones as well.

Gaslighting

Blame-shifting - Gaslighters use the blame-shifting technique regularly in their interactions with victims. All conversations and events are twisted in such a way that invariably, the blame for all the wrong consequences fall on you. Even when they have to explain their incorrigible behavior, they will say it happened because of something you did or said. Slowly but surely, gaslighters will make their targets believe that they are responsible and accountable for all the wrong things happening in their lives.

Isolating the victim - The gaslighter likes to corner his or her victim in such a way that there are no exits left. Moreover, if the victim has people who offer love and support during difficult times, then it becomes difficult for the abuser to control his or her life. The gaslighter works hard to make sure that he or she is the only reference point for the victim, and all other perspectives are closed.

One of the most effective ways this situation is achieved is through the isolation of the victim. Manipulators lie about your friends and family to turn you against them. Conveniently, only the manipulators will know about secrets about the people that they want you to hate. Repeated feeding of misinformation will lead you to a

Illusion vs. Reality

point where you will trust only the manipulator. When this condition is reached, you are in total surrender mode.

Using a mask of assertiveness or fake compassion - This masked behavior of abusers makes you believe that you have got it all wrong. They will say that they did not mean anything close to what you have interpreted from the interaction. You begin to believe them so much so that you doubt your own thinking process and accept their version as the true one and yours as the imagined one because you think you are going crazy. Here are illustrative statements commonly used by gaslighters:

- You know how much I love you and will never do anything to cause you any pain.

- You recall the time I stayed up with you the entire night when you were not well? Doesn't that mean anything? Doesn't that make you realize how much I love and care for you? (It would have been one instance when such a thing happened!)

- You are the most important person in my life, and I cannot live without you.

While these words seem loving and affectionate, the trick lies in the follow-up action. Ask yourself if the person's actions and behaviors are aligned with the true meaning of these words. Or are they simply hollow and fake words?

Manipulative Techniques Resembling Attention-Seeking Behaviors

Some manipulators are so smart that they end up using attention-seeking behaviors and attitudes to manipulate and control others. You would think that the manipulator was only throwing a tantrum and give in to his or her rantings. If you are not careful about repeatedly falling for this gimmick, you are likely to fall into the trap of manipulation very soon. Beware of the following attention-seeking behaviors that are actually disguised manipulative techniques.

Hysterical behavior - If an individual is reacting hysterically and creating histrionic outbursts to anything and everything around him or her, then you could be facing the threat of manipulation from this person. Typically, such outbursts are highly melodramatic and exaggerated. These kinds of attention-seeking outbursts are commonly used by manipulators to get what they want from you because you are caught in a highly embarrassing situation where everyone around is looking at you as if you are obliged to solve the manipulator's problem.

Playing the victim - Manipulators use the status of being a victim to appear above others. They may never have had a big problem in life. But their ability to convert the smallest issues into something big and describe how victimized they felt gets them a lot of attention. Through this habit of attention-seeking, these manipulators are skilled at viewing everything happening to them in a negative light, empowering them to get into the role of a victim all the time. Most people, especially gentle-hearted people who are easy manipulation targets, fall for these gimmicks, and actually, end up being the victim.

Playing the role of an indispensable friend - Manipulators have this amazing talent of playing the role of an indispensable friend and squeezing their way into the lives of vulnerable and weak people. The role of an indispensable friend is highly suited for manipulators as it gives them a status higher than others in the victim's life.

However, with time and concerted effort from the manipulator's side, these poor victims become so dependent on the manipulators that they end up getting exploited to the hilt. If a sensible person manages to see through such gimmicks and gets out of the clutches of such 'indispensable friends,' then these manipulators get nasty and disrespectful.

Pretending to be sick - Sickness is one of the most effective attention-seeking methods used by manipulators. As it is natural for people to feel sorry for sick people, most manipulators who use this technique quickly achieve their ends.

Manipulators tend to use either imaginary health problems or an existing issue (which is more likely to cause little or no harm) to garner attention for themselves in order to control people in their lives. In fact, some manipulators can go to the extent of harming themselves to seek attention and sympathy.

This attention-seeking method is usually adopted by introverted manipulators who are not skilled at other forms of manipulation. Such people resort to subtler means of gaining attention than those who use hysterics and drama. It is still as dangerous as any other form of manipulation.

Pretending to be busy all the time - There are people who pretend to be continuously busy and keep telling you that they wish they had an easy life like yours. This kind of manipulation tactic not only gets the attention but also puts down the victim who ends up feeling guilty for having an 'easy' life. Sooner rather than later, this manipulator has the victim dancing to his or her tunes.

Munchausen Syndrome by Proxy (MSBP) - This form of manipulation tactic is highly dangerous because it is triggered by a mental illness where the manipulator will actually cause harm to the victim (many times, serious harm), and then step in at the last minute as a savior to the victim. The ultimate purpose of this method is for the manipulator to get the glory and success that comes after the 'rescue.' Of course, the victim feels obliged to his or her rescuer and ends up in complete control of the manipulator.

It is important to note that this kind of gaslighting technique can actually be very dangerous as the intention to cause harm in the first place could go awry and end in fatality too. Imagine a manipulator using the tactic to trip a victim down a long flight of stairs thinking that he or she will quickly take the victim to the hospital, which would be seen as a rescue. It is highly possible that the victim could bang his or her head on the way down, and get irreparably injured or fatally wounded, right? The manipulators are really not in control of their actions in such cases.

The Key Elements of Gaslighting Success

Yes, the stealth and the subtlety of gaslighting tactics make it very difficult to identify and recognize this kind of dangerously manipulative behavior. Here are some key elements to help you break down your understanding of how gaslighters achieve success in their evil plans:

They undermine their victims stealthily and subtly - Stealth and subtlety are the foundation of gaslighting behavior. Gaslighters are such great liars that they can mess with the minds of their victims in such confounding and confusing ways that the hapless target cannot really detect that he or she is being manipulated. They use fake compassion and camouflaged affection, which tend to make the victims believe that they are being cared for and not manipulated in any way.

They are excellent deflectors of arguments and objections - Gaslighters are skilled at deflecting arguments and objections that victims raise. They brush aside victims' arguments lightheartedly and casually. They will say things like, 'What rubbish! Have you had problems sleeping recently? Have you taken your medication?' These statements are more likely to get the victim looking at their own mistakes rather than thinking they are being manipulated, right?

Illusion vs. Reality

Manipulators make the victims question everything they believed was true - The ultimate goal of gaslighters is to get the victims to question their own reality. Gaslighters achieve this final purpose in stages. They start small and slowly and steadily reach a stage where their victims doubt every aspect of their lives and experiences.

- Phase 1 - Helena's boyfriend, Ben, began by telling her, 'You're not tired. You have had a good amount of sleep.' It is harmless enough to agree with Ben, right?

- Phase 2 - Ben says, 'Come, come, Helena. Now, you are trying to escape from your responsibility. How can you say you are tired after sleeping for more than 10 hours last night?' Now, the guilt in Helena's mind takes shape.

- Phase 3 - Ben says, 'You said the same thing last week too, and yet, you were able to sit and watch a movie without sleeping. If you could watch the movie, you could not have been tired. Are you trying to keep something from me?' Helena immediately jumps up and does what Ben wants her to do feeling totally guilty for having watched a movie instead of doing what her boyfriend told her to.

- Phase 4 - Ben's words have become sharper and stronger than before, and his demands from Helena are becoming increasingly difficult. But, Helena believes that he has her best interests at heart and does not think that Ben could be manipulating her in any way.

The above phases might happen over a few months, or sometimes, even over an entire year. There could have been a few occasions when Ben allowed Helena to have the benefit of the doubt. However, he made sure that such occasions were completely leveraged to his advantage in making sure Helena was under his total control!

Differences between Manipulation and Bad Behavior

Many times, especially for people who have already undergone the trauma of being gaslighting victims, it can get very difficult to discern between manipulative narcissism and simply bad behavior that is not only harmless but also can be cured easily. It is important to know the difference so that you don't lose out on a potentially good relationship and also to ensure that innocent people are not mistaken for being gaslighters merely due to their inability to behave nicely.

People who behave badly don't do it repeatedly, and there is hardly ever a discernible pattern that can be clearly seen. Lying occasionally because of embarrassment or guilt or genuine and occasional disagreements or even a perspective that is completely different from yours, cannot be categorized as manipulative behavior. Keep a lookout for a pattern that adds up to something dangerous or sinister, and if you come across such people, then you need to have your antennae up and alert. The others need not worry you excessively.

Keep a lookout for all the tell-tale and warning signs mentioned in this chapter so that you can quickly and effectively identify gaslighters who are trying to control you and your life. Yes, some may seem like a harmless annoyance. Yet, continue to watch and observe any suspicious activity and seek help or run when you realize that you are in any kind of a relationship with a manipulator. Learn to discern between illusion and reality and don't allow a manipulator to take this power away from you.

Gaslighting

CHAPTER 3

Manipulation Where it is Least Expected

One of the biggest misunderstandings about gaslighting is it is a manipulative strategy that exists only between romantically involved partners. Well, I hope by the time you read this chapter, you will have accepted that this is not the case, and know that gaslighting is not restricted to any one kind of relationship. It can be seen everywhere and anywhere.

Gaslighting in Families

The scary thing about gaslighting occurring in parent-child relationships is that it is treated as normal behavior, and mostly accepted as being okay by society. It is believed that parents will never want anything but the best for their children, and therefore, any kind of behavior is allowed. To be brutally honest, this thought process is archaic and unscientific and has no logical foundation.

First, not all parents have the intention of the ultimate good for their kids. It would be naive to think that there are no parents who have abused and misused the power of parenthood, causing emotional, mental, and physical harm to their own kids. Moreover, even if the parents did have their kids' best interests at heart, gaslighting techniques would hardly be used to prove parental love.

Additionally, gaslighting in parenthood, regardless of true intent, can cause far more harm and good. The harmful effects can easily spill into the child's adult life. Such children tend to grow up with trust issues. They get very low self-confidence levels considering they have never been allowed to think, talk, and make decisions for themselves. Such kids invariably don't allow themselves the freedom to be independent because they doubt their capabilities.

Having said all that, it is equally important to remember that just strictness and discipline cannot be misinterpreted as gaslighting techniques. Like the suggestion made in the previous chapter, look out for abnormal patterns in behavior and then decide whether it is gaslighting that is happening or simple love, affection, and disciplinary behavior being displayed, perhaps, a bit overwhelmingly. Here are some lookout signs you can use:

Gaslighting parents tell you what to like and dislike - Here are some examples:

- What do you mean you don't like steak? Our whole family loves steak. There is not a single member who doesn't love his or her steak. Now, come on, shut up with your complaining and eat it up. And didn't you eat steak and enjoy it last Monday?

- Don't you like the beach? Now, what kind of dislike is that? Everyone in our family loves the beach. C'mon, get ready for the beach holiday this summer. It is going to be as much fun as the one that happened last summer.

Do you see the pattern? Such parents refuse to accept that their child could be different from them and others in the family. Tastes and preferences are natural and cannot be enforced. However, parents of this kind use such tactics to keep control over their children.

If your parents never allow you to like or dislike things that are not aligned with their choices, then it might be important for you to point out this discrepancy and see how the discussion goes.

Gaslighting parents don't really care for the happiness of their children - Parents using gaslighting techniques rarely try to solve the problems of their children. Not only this, they simply don't accept that the child has a problem at all in the first place. Parents use this excuse not to help their kids find happiness. Telling their children that crying is not for boys (yes, especially boys) is a way of dismissing the issues the child is facing.

Instructing children to 'hide' their feelings because showing emotions is not a civilized thing to do is a common way of brushing kids' problems under the carpet. If you see such an unrelenting behavioral pattern, then you could be dealing with a gaslighting parent.

They treat all your ideas as 'silly' - Parents commonly use this tactic to cover up their own ignorance. Power dynamics invariably play a big parent in a parent-child relationship, and accepting ignorance does not come easily to some parents. The child's ideas (particularly the ones that the parents cannot understand) are dismissed as silly and childish.

Imagine this situation. A much-loved dog in the family has just died, and the child is distraught shedding copious tears. His sadness is deep. In such a situation, if the father were to say, 'I don't know why you are making such a silly issue of it. Anyway, you did not like the dog very much. Don't simply shed crocodile tears to impress people. I was the one who loved the dog more than you and looked after him. You should be ashamed that you are doing so little to help me.'

In one sweep, the child's feelings have been completely invalidated, and that poor kid will think that his tears are getting in the way of his father's happiness and feel guilty about his feelings. Also, the father has made it very clear that he, as a parent, is the more important member of the relationship.

Sometimes, parents use the term 'wild imagination' to dismiss the ideas and thoughts of their kids. Children brought up on a staple of such behavior find it exceedingly difficult to try out their ideas and, with time, even lose the ability to think on their own for fear of ridicule.

Gaslighting parents are always right, and the kids are always wrong - Parents employing gaslighting techniques never accept that they can be wrong. They insist that the kids are wrong and they themselves are always right. And the only 'evidence' to them being right is that they are older and wiser than the children. Of course, you have to be careful of name-calling because in some cases they could really be right. To reiterate an earlier point, remember to look for a pattern of negative and manipulative behavior.

A supportive parent is one who works hard to keep their children happy and healthy regardless of power dynamics and ego issues. It is extremely unfortunate that children are particularly vulnerable to gaslighting, considering that they look up to their parents for their opinions and perspectives. Manipulative parents commonly punish their children for real and imagined mistakes, and the poor child grows up believing that he or she is incapable of being right.

Here is a simple example that can be the initial stages of manipulative parent strategy. The mother yells at Sam in the morning, 'See, you are going to be late for school again. If you simply did what you were being told to you instead of mucking around, you are going to have this problem every day.' Sam is going to believe this statement whether he is in the wrong or not, and in the future, his perceptions and beliefs are going to be warped and totally messed up. He is going to be under the control of his mother all through his life.

Gaslighting by Adult Children

Even though this can be categorized under 'gaslighting in families,' it makes sense to give it a separate heading considering how common this problem is around the world. Adult children can be master manipulators taking advantage of their desperate parents who always try hard to keep their children happy. Adult children are masters at using guilt to manipulate their older parents. Here are a couple of examples:

- Oh! So, you won't help me? Then, I am going to land on the street and get killed by someone.

- You keep telling me to work hard and get a job. Stop pressuring me. I cannot do this, and if you don't back off, I might just kill myself.

Gaslighting

The frustrated parent(s) feels so guilty that he or she gives in to all the unreasonable demands of the adult child. Here are some ways that adult children hold their parents to ransom to get what they want:

Adult children use emotional blackmail - The child will threaten to kill himself or herself if parents don't give in. While genuine problematic cases where the person is not in the right frame of mind and can cause self-harm should be taken seriously, repeated pressure tactics of self-harm require to be handled firmly. As a responsible parent, you must put your foot down when you know that these tactics are ways to run away from accountability.

Your child is lying using selective memory - You clearly remember having an important conversation about something with your child. You also remember the promise that he or she made to you. But, suddenly, your child recalls that conversation in an entirely new light. He or she is twisting it to make it appear the exact opposite of what happened. Your child is extremely good with selective memory techniques and conveniently forgets certain vital elements that could alter the meaning and outcome of the conversation drastically. If you see this repeatedly, then you know you are being manipulated by your adult child.

Manipulation Where it is Least Expected

You are dealing with all the problems of your adult child - Thanks to your adult child's inertia and complete lack of responsibility, in your old age, you are taking on a second job so you can feed an extra mouth, you are bearing your child's debts, etc. Your child's responsibilities have become yours while he or she continues to behave irresponsibly without a care in the world. If this is the case in your life, then you know you are being taken for a sucker by your adult child.

Your adult child is continually borrowing money from you - You are helping your child financially month in and month out. He or she might call it 'borrowing,' but, you haven't got a penny back from your child. All this is because your adult child is so lazy that he or she cannot work hard and keep a consistent job, and needs a new job every few months. While helping your child with money occasionally is fine, exploiting you is not! It is nothing short of manipulative behavior.

You do not expect respect any more - This situation is when you have almost reached the ultimate purpose of your manipulative adult child. After repeated attempts at trying to get your child to change, you have finally given up so much that you don't even expect respect from him or her anymore. Remember to get out of the rut before you reach this stage of no-return.

Gaslighting in Relationships

There is little doubt that gaslighting is highly prevalent in romantic relationships of all kinds, including married, unmarried, live-in, same-sex, and more. Here are a few illustrations to help you understand how manipulative controls work in any relationship.

Example 1 - Your partner may have promised you that he will get something done for you on Saturday. When you try to remind him via text message or phone call, the manipulative person is likely to say, 'No silly, I said Sunday, not Saturday. I'm busy the whole of Saturday.'

By itself, this statement is quite harmless and cannot really be called gaslighting. In fact, it is likely you misheard or misinterpreted the meaning. However, the same thing is repeated for an unreasonable number of times, and then you need to start questioning your status in the relationship.

Example 2 - You had chosen a Thai restaurant for your anniversary dinner because you heard your girlfriend say she loves Thai. But, a manipulative person would like to respond in the following way, 'I don't particularly like Thai cuisine. But, I know of one great Mexican restaurant that we must try.'

You begin to doubt what you had heard earlier. Did she say she liked or disliked Thai food? Manipulative people use this technique of saying one thing and then backtracking to shame you or make you feel guilty of not paying attention in conversations.

Example 3 - Look at the following conversation where the gaslighting technique has reached deep levels, and your manipulative partner is actually making you believe that you are backtracking on an already agreed condition.

- You: I am so excited about us going to meet my partners for the Easter weekend. They are dying to see you.

- Your partner: Didn't we agree that we will wait for a little while longer before we meet your people?

- You: We spoke last week, and you said you are perfectly ready to meet with them.

- Your partner: We did speak, and I said I'd be happy to meet them. But I also said, let's do it after a month. But, now that you have already told them, I can't do anything but come. I don't want to disappoint your family.

You see the way the episode is panning out? It now seems that your partner is accommodating your mistake, which automatically puts you on the defensive. Such people will keep this instance in mind and will use to control an important decision in the future.

Gaslighting at the Workplace

Gaslighting at the workplace is all about keeping and holding power. Here are a couple of illustrations to help you understand gaslighting tactics commonly employed at the workplace.

Example 1 - Suppose you go to your boss to report that you have completed a given task, a manipulative person is likely to respond like this, 'Why did you waste your time doing that thing when I told him specifically to do this task?'

Now, any average person is going to get agitated with this comment, and you will respond in a fumbling, or perhaps, angry tone. Your manipulative boss is going to say, 'Aren't you overreacting to this just a wee bit more than necessary? Now, go and work on that other task.'

Example 2 - You are sure to connect with classic workplace gaslighting tactic. Suppose your boss promised you a raise the coming May. You approach him or her promptly and remind him just before the pay rises are to be decided. Your boss says this, 'I didn't promise you a raise. I only said that you could get a raise if your performance gets better. Sadly to say, there are many elements still lacking in that aspect.' You know you have been taken for a ride.

Example 3 - A colleague of yours is trying hard to get one-up on you. She makes you jittery with statements like, 'I heard that the boss is not very happy with your report. I am sure you are in trouble.' The colleague walks away knowing full well that she has sown the seeds of self-doubt in your mind.

If you fought back a bit, this person would respond with, 'I only wanted to warn you so that you can be prepared. God! Someone is really feeling very sensitive today.'

Example 4 - Another colleague-triggered gaslighting statement could go something like this, 'Weren't you marked on that mail? Well, maybe the boss doesn't yet trust you with such important things, I suppose.'

Gaslighting tactics at the workplace can also happen through actions and are not restricted to verbal abuse. Your colleague could come and shut down your computer simply without reason. It is quite likely that you forgot to save your work at that time. Imagine the pain and agony.

Alternately, he or she could move an important file from the place you normally keep it to another place, and it takes a bit of time for you to find it. This loss of time might happen exactly when your boss is demanding that file right now. Your boss is not likely to take your 'tardiness' lightly. Although you don't have proof, deep down, you feel that something is not right.

And yet, all these instances add up and create weakness, fear, and self-doubt in your mind. You believe you are not worthy of your job, and sooner rather than later, you could simply call it quits. Beware of such situations!

Gaslighting in Public Life and Politics

Politicians all over the world are known to use gaslighting tactics to control how they are viewed by the public. For example, in a speech on July 2018, Trump lashed out at his imagined opponents for 'distorting, doctoring, and fudging' his tape using advanced technology to make him look bad in the public eye. He refused to back down on these allegations even when journalists published the entire transcript and the untampered full video.

What was Trump doing? He was making the public question their own experiences so that they felt confused and confounded and didn't know what to believe. He was making the public doubt their memories, realities, and perception by sowing the seeds of confusion. If this is not gaslighting, then what else can it be called?

Moreover, this is not the first time Trump is believed to have been using gaslighting tactics to confound the American public. The use of Russian intelligence and intervention to affect voting patterns in the 2016 presidential election was also dismissed as 'fake.' Trump knows that for an uninformed public, it just comes down to his word against the word of ordinary journalists who are out to 'defame and demean' him in the public eye.

Therefore, gaslighting is not restricted to being between two people. One person with the backing of political and financial strength can gaslight an entire nation.

Gaslighting

Just a Friendly Reminder...

I'd like to offer you this amazing resource which my clients pay for. It is a report I written when I first began my journey.

Click on the picture above or navigate to the website below to join my exclusive email list. Upon joining, you will receive this incredible report on how to recognize an abusive relationship.

Gaslighting

If you ask most people on the street what an abusive relationship is, chances are you'd get a description of physical abuse. And yes, that is most certainly an abusive relationship. However, abuse comes in many forms. The actual meaning of abuse is when someone exerts control over another person.

Find out more about recognizing an abusive relationship and learn how to take control over your life by clicking on the book above or by going to this link:

http://tinyurl.com/RecognizeAbusiveRelationship

CHAPTER 4

They're Not All the Same

Gaslighting and manipulative techniques are one thing, and the types of manipulators is another thing. Each person has a predominant technique that he or she uses on their victims, and the choice is dependent on multiple factors including the purpose for controlling the victim, the personalities of the manipulator and/or the target, the situation, and many more. Let us look at the different types of manipulators you are likely to encounter.

The Manipulator Who Uses Guilt

The manipulator who makes you take a guilt trip is, perhaps, one of the most dangerous gaslighting practitioners in the world. Here are some classic statements the 'guilt builders' employ on their victims:

- If you were a good child, you would listen to your mama.

- If you truly loved me, you would not say no.

- If you really understood what I have gone through, you would not speak to me like this.

- If you were a good husband, you would never refuse my request.

They fill the victims' minds with self-guilt and make them pliable. Then, such guilt builders enforce their main ideas and thoughts on the highly vulnerable victim. Nothing works like guilt to turn on a repenting attitude, and manipulators want their victims to show repentance so that they can use it to their advantage.

What happens when you repent? It means you are sorry and are prepared for punishment, which is a perfect situation for them to start controlling you and your mind. Such manipulators blame you for all the wrong things, including their own behavior. For example, 'If you hadn't said that nasty thing, I would not have behaved as badly as I did.' So, their bad behavior becomes your problem.

The ones who cannot take responsibility for anything in their lives are the ones who typically use guilt building tactic to control others. This kind of manipulative behavior is based primarily on emotionally weak people who are ready to take responsibility for real and imagined faults to be accepted by the manipulator.

Manipulators who use guilt tend to carry their emotional scars like a badge showing it off to everyone so that they can control the people around them. Here are some common words or situations used by this type of manipulator to make you guilty:

- I have had such a bad childhood.

- You don't know the amount of pain I went through looking after my sick father.

- I have had to put up with your horrible father, and you simply don't know what I have sacrificed for your sake.

- You are angry because I am not ready for commitment. But, you don't know how difficult it is for me considering that I suffered loneliness after my father abandoned me.

The Aggressive Manipulator or 'Threatener'

The most common forms of abuse perpetrated by the aggressive or threatening kind of manipulator is domestic abuse. Here are some classic lines that this kind of manipulator will spew from his or her mouth:

- I will beat you black and blue if you don't give me the money.

- I will kill you if you don't listen to me.

- I will throw you onto the streets if you don't heed my words.

- I will not give you food if you don't complete your homework on time.

People who have a lot of physical and mental strength generally tend to use this kind of manipulation tactic. They are confident of the fear they can instill in the victim using whichever method they can to get their work done. The 'threatener' will threaten to destroy your career, family, relationships, and more.

They're Not All the Same

'Threateners' are great blackmailers who tend to take advantage of the secret information they have on others to control people. The thing about this type of manipulator is that they may be strong physically, and yet, they lack the courage to do things in the open. They tend to hide their aggressive behavior and will display it only in front of their victims and no one else.

The deep sense of fear created by 'threateners' can be powerful enough to drive victims to do their bidding,the including getting gaslighted. 'Threateners' also tend to isolate their victims from supportive family and friends. Being isolated like this makes victims surrender themselves entirely to the mercy of 'threateners.'

The most evident sense of fear is rooted in being physically abused by this type of manipulator. It is imperative that you do everything in your power to steer clear of such manipulators as their aggression can lead to fatality too.

While the physical threat is one way to manipulate, subtle forms of threats are also employed by manipulators. For example, a wife who wants to control her husband's diet might say, 'If you continue to eat this way, you can rest assured that in less than six months, you will look at a huge drum.' Here, the wife wants to control the eating habits of her husband. She uses this threat as a way of controlling one aspect of her husband's life. It's likely that the wife hates to see her husband's happy face when he eats and wants to wipe that pleasure from his life.

The Manipulator Who Uses the Silent Treatment

The ones who are not smart enough to get you on a guilt trip or be aggressive tend to use the silent treatment to manipulate. This type of manipulation is most effective when you, as the victim, desperately need the help of the manipulator. Such manipulative techniques withdraw all kinds of communication and contact with the victim until their desires are achieved.

When it comes to romantically involved partners, then this type of manipulator will withdraw even sex from the equation. In fact, women manipulators tend to play this card to control their male partners knowing full well that some men need sex like food and water!

A silent treatment manipulation is a powerful form of emotional abuse as it negatively affects the very basic need of human beings to be in touch with others. The silent treatment is meant to instill a fear of getting disconnected with the manipulator in the minds of the victims. It is also generally used by people in the initial stages of romantic relationships. The controlling partner would have used charm and fake compassion to build the necessary connection, and then turn on the silent treatment to start and deepen the controlling effect.

When faced with the silent treatment suddenly, the victim feels the fear of rejection and abandonment and will do anything to win back favor with the manipulator. The silent treatment giver can result in utterly frustrating the victim. There are many reasons why people use the silent treatment method, including:

- It makes them take the 'high moral road' giving them the upper hand in any relationship.

- Other methods of showing their displeasure have not produced their desired outcomes.

- It is easy to defend this kind of behavior later on. All that needs to be said is, 'I said nothing,' and wash off all blame and accountability in the relationship.

Examples, where silent treatment manipulators work effectively are:

- A mother ignoring her child

- Silent treatment on online platforms
- Nonverbal show of anger like throwing things randomly
- Keeping a colleague out of a collaborative project

The Manipulator Who Attacks Your Self-Esteem

This type of manipulator attacks your self-esteem by:

- Putting you down
- Labeling you
- Passing judgments
- Showing contempt

The self-esteem attackers do everything they can to criticize you and make you feel inferior. The worst thing is that these verbal attacks need not be direct. If someone tells you, ''Only working women wear lipstick during the day,' it translates to telling you that you are a whore, doesn't it?

It is extremely important to be very wary of such kinds of manipulators because they are highly skilled at discrediting you among you family and friends. This kind

They're Not All the Same

of manipulator expects you to surrender and give in to their control to avoid being belittled and shamed.

Here are some tell-tale signs to warn you if you are associated with a self-esteem attacker:

- You are always in a state of self-doubt, practically on a daily basis.

- You are always in comparison mode, comparing yourself and your capabilities with others and their achievements.

- You don't know how to take compliments and praise from others. Moreover, you don't appreciate your accomplishments and achievements. In fact, you minimize what you have achieved, even big achievements.

- You have no idea of your strengths and personality assets.

- You are scared to explore new possibilities and experiences. This fear is so deeply ingrained that you don't mind staying in a rut but will not attempt new ventures regardless of anything.

- You avoid attending social meetings and even keep interactions with your family and friends to a minimum.

All the signs mentioned above are directly connected to the fact that your self-esteem is under attack. Find out if these effects are the result of manipulators in your life. The self-esteem attacker uses this method because not only does he or she get to control victims but is also able to do it without physical violence and aggression.

The Manipulator Who Uses Competition

Can you recall the effects of the following statements?

- Let me see who will be the first to get ready for school?

- Whoever gets me the newspaper will become papa's favorite?

- Whoever finishes lunch first will get a surprise gift from mama?

Although they might seem innocuous, many parents use these competitive-driven statements to control their children. In fact, most of us were subjected to these competitions with our siblings during our childhood, right? Most parents, perhaps, don't even realize that they are using gaslighting techniques in such cases.

Most of them use this method simply because parenting becomes easy. They forget that if there is a winner, then there is a loser in the bargain, and being a winner or loser could result in long-term harmful consequences. Also, being in a competitive spirit at all times can cause a lot of psychological harm that will be carried forward into adulthood.

Even in other kinds of relationships, the competitive manipulator makes an appearance. For example, a manipulative husband might tell his wife that if she cooks her best meal for dinner for his friends, then he will buy her a nice piece of jewelry. A manipulative woman who knows that her boyfriend has self-confidence issues could say, 'I don't know if I want to spend this coming weekend with you or Jim. I think it depends on who will buy me the most beautiful pair of earrings.'

In an office environment too, these kinds of manipulators can be found. The boss will tell his team, 'The one who brings me the best presentation will be given a chance to travel with me to Paris for the upcoming business trip.' Yes, setting such competitions is a great way to get employees to give their best. However, if someone is doing it repeatedly, then it is likely to be a manipulative gesture to control his or team rather than to bring out the best in people.

Manipulators use the competition element not only because it is easy for them but also because they are obsessed with catfights. Even when there is no need for competition, such manipulators will bring it on just to satisfy their own cravings. Use these differences to help you discern between healthy competition and manipulation:

Manipulative people:

- Withhold critical information as collateral to achieve their desires

- Wield their power and control over others

- Twist the emotions and feelings of other people to achieve their own ends

- Want others to fail so that they come across as winners

- Use fear and guilt to motivate people to do their bidding

Competitive people:

- Use their power to empower others around them and help others achieve success

- Do not hold back information that can be used by everyone to achieve success

- Employ their own emotional intelligence to help others in need of emotional support

- Use positive reinforcement to motivate employees and team members

- Encourage a collaborative approach within their teams

The Manipulator Who Uses Criticism

This type of manipulator finds fault with everything you do. They use criticism and fault-finding mechanisms to wreck your confidence levels. When you continue to receive criticism from someone for everything you do, sooner rather than later, you are likely to lose your sense of self-reliance, which makes it easy for the manipulator to control you. You are repeatedly made to feel inferior.

And finally, it reaches such a stage that you are ready to surrender yourself to the manipulator in the hope that criticisms come to a halt. Psychology experts say that indulging in constant criticism is a deadly form of emotional abuse.

An indirect form of criticism that this type of manipulators uses is sarcasm. In fact, criticizing manipulator like all other types of manipulators prefers to work in an underhanded manner and avoid direct confrontation. Using sarcasm comes in very useful for such subtle occasions.

The criticizing manipulator becomes a self-proclaimed judge of your life and everything in it. Through repeated conversations, such people suddenly look like your 'spiritual guide' to you and to everyone around you. You don't take any decision in your life without running it through such manipulators. These people are skilled at telling you how you must lead your life.

In fact, criticizing manipulator uses a lot of philosophy to explain how you must lead your life. They will use reams of philosophical quotes and maxims and give your detailed step-by-step instructions on how to live your life. The worst part is that if things don't turn out as they 'promised' you, even then you will be blamed. They will find some tiny flaw in the way you handled the situation because of which the outcome was not as they predicted!

Sarcastic is a powerful weapon in the hands of criticizing manipulators. For example, they will not call you a dog, but they will offer you a bone! Criticizers use sarcasm to demean and devalue your thoughts, opinions, and all aspects of your life. For example, they could send you a message like, 'Maybe if you read a little more, you could have more distinguished friends.' In this case, the manipulator is finding fault with your friends indirectly. He or she wants you to disconnect with some or all of your friends in a bid to isolate you. This message could work for some of us who are very sensitive to criticism.

We are likely to look at our friends through new eyes and find the faults that the manipulator wants us to find. Consequently, we begin to think that the manipulator is right, and we are wrong. This way, criticizing manipulator controls who should be your friend and who should not.

Here is an illustration of how a manipulative husband who uses criticism to his advantage. Jane, the wife of the manipulative husband, Jim, has caught him cheating on her. She shows him the motel bill that she found in his wallet. Instead of focusing on his affair, he turns around and yells at her for going through his wallet. He raves and rants about the importance of trust in a marriage, and tells her that her act of searching his wallet undermines the trust he had in her. He criticizes her for her distrustful behavior.

Soon, poor Jane has become so caught up with his criticisms of her attitude that the affair is forgotten, and she starts to focus on her mistake. She begins to feel guilty about searching his wallet, and within a few minutes, starts to ask for forgiveness for her 'rash' behavior. The cheating ends up like a simple misunderstanding that she should never have brought to his attention at all.

The Manipulator Who Uses Charm

This type of manipulator starts with the act of charming you because they know that in order to ride a horse, the poor animal needs to be first stroked lovingly. Initially, the charmer manipulator lays on his or her charm nice and thickly through pleasant and disarming behavior.

These manipulators will flatter you and entertain you with their conversations and talk. They are invariably witty people who can make you laugh a lot. They pretend to be

They're Not All the Same

highly sensitive to your needs and expectations. All this charming attitude is the first stage of manipulation.

Once the charmer knows he or she has control over you, then the personality undergoes a drastic change. They start the manipulation process slowly and soon, thanks to their charm, you are in their complete control. The web of seduction that the charmers spin around you masks your objectivity, and you see everything through their eyes.

The charmer is not only witty but can be a great talker and conversationalist. They are great at changing topics too. For example, if they are talking to you about one topic and they get a whiff of the conversation not going their way, they will subtly and seamlessly change the topic to something else that is more suited to their needs. You won't even realize it until it's too late to do anything.

Here's an example. They will laugh at your attire and say, 'You look like a penguin in that dress.' When they see your hurt face, they will quickly say, 'Oh! I didn't realize you were becoming so sensitive these days.' The apology for hurting you is completely forgotten, and the topic has been changed from your 'penguin-looking' dress to your sensitivity which immediately puts you on the defensive, not to mention the fact that you might look at yourself in the mirror and actually find a penguin looking back at you!

Even if you had chosen to confront them with their insulting behavior, they are likely to change the topic to something else that has nothing to do with the insult. The apology didn't come at all, and you have also either forgotten it or simply taken it as a joke. That is the power of charmers. They will say nasty things to you and not just get away with it but also make you believe that they were right.

You see all the actions of the charmer as good because they show you what they want you to see. They conveniently and unobtrusively distract you so much that you cannot view them as being wrong and manipulative. You readily and wholeheartedly accept taking their side with regard to all your decisions and perspectives without realizing that you are being enslaved.

Whatever the type of manipulation used, the ultimate purpose of gaslighters is to control their victims so that they lose their sense of reality and life.

CHAPTER 5

Victim vs. Manipulator

An interesting fact is the manipulative tactics affect not only the victim but the manipulator too. Yes, the victim undergoes indescribable pain and agony and might even go crazy. However, the manipulator also feels the effects of his or her manipulative attitude. Knowing all sides of the manipulation cycle will help you deal with situations in a better way.

For example, if you realize that your husband is using manipulation to cover his sense of inferiority complex, it might be possible to help him overcome his problems, which, in turn, will help you become free of his nasty ways. So, read on and equip yourself with more knowledge to handle situations in an improved way.

Effects of Manipulation on the Victims

Manipulation can have short-term and long-term effects on the victim.

Short-term effects - In the initial days of being victims of manipulation, people feel confused, anxious, and uncertain. Here are some more details about the short-term effects of manipulation on the victims:

Confusion and surprise - Victims are confused as to what is happening with them, or in a particular relationship. They cannot understand what went wrong. The confounding thoughts that run through their minds are, 'What happened that made someone who was kind and warm with me turn against me? Why is he or she behaving like a total stranger?'

Self-questioning sets in - If you are the victim, you begin to question yourself a lot, right? Did you imagine what happened or is something wrong with you? Did you hear or see correctly, or were you dreaming? This self-questioning is a result of the manipulator's behavior that is telling you that you are wrong, and he or she is right.

Anxious and vigilant - Victims feel anxious and extra vigilant as to what is happening with them in the hope of preventing unpleasant situations arising in their lives. They are scared of making the slightest mistake, which might rock the boat in any way whatsoever. Also, they scan for behavioral signs in their manipulator's actions and words to try and gauge if an outburst is about to take place. Victims feel they are walking on eggshells at all times because they have to be extra careful of what they say and how they behave as they don't want to trigger nastiness in the manipulator.

Guilt and shame - Victims start feeling guilty and are ashamed that they are responsible for the presence of manipulation in their lives. Moreover, the manipulator starts using blame to enhance control over victims, which only increases the sense of guilt and shame in the minds of victims.

Passivity sets in - Victims notice that any action from their end leads to added emotional and psychological pain. Therefore, they prefer to be quiet which slowly but steadily leads to passivity in all aspects of their lives.

Becoming passive and accepting the pain without reaction or response becomes the norm. Additionally, victims tend to make themselves smaller or invisible by avoiding eye contact with people they meet or even avoiding social contact altogether.

Long-term effects - As victims continue in a manipulative relationship, the effects change and harden over time, and some of them undergo such huge personality changes that friends from their earlier social circles (before being subjected to manipulation) can hardly even recognize them. Here are some of the long-term effects of manipulation that can cause utter devastation in the lives of hapless victims:

You feel utterly lonely and desolate - Over time, you can become numb to everything that is happening around you. Even in the most joyful moments, you lose the connection with your own emotions. Slowly, you only end up observing what is happening in your life rather than living it. You feel utterly lonely, hopeless, and desolate.

You always need approval before doing anything - The manipulator has controlled your mind so much that it is not your own anymore. Therefore, you lose the ability to make decisions for yourself. You always look out for an approval from the manipulator (or someone else, if he or she has dumped you and moved on) to decide even on simple things like what to wear, eat, etc.

Another manifestation of this dire need for outside approval is that you end up being a people pleaser. You are always looking for ways to keep people happy, even if you have to suffer a lot into the bargain. You could be a person who wants to look the best and want everyone to appreciate your appearance. In fact, dressing up becomes an obsession to the point that you refuse to go out if you don't have anything nice to wear. It is a clear sign of being controlled by a manipulator who kept telling you about your inadequacies. Consequently, you are always working to appear perfect in front of other people.

You could have depressive and anxiety disorders - Your nervous system has been under the constant strain of stress and anxiety. In the long run, this is most likely to have a drastic effect on your mind. Depression and anxiety disorders are common mental ailments in long-term victims of manipulation.

You become highly judgmental - You learn from and copy your manipulator's behavior and attitude. So, if you have been under the influence of a manipulator who had a judgmental attitude, then you are likely to become one yourself. Always being seen through a colored lens makes you believe that it is the only way to see things in the world.

Moreover, your manipulator's expectations from you were always sky high. In turn, you expect the same from others too, and look deep and long to find faults in the people in your life. Being judgmental becomes a form of control for you.

You become resentful - Resentfulness becomes a buzzword in your life in the long-term. After being treated badly by the manipulator for a long time, you end up focusing only on the bad behavior of everyone in your life. You find it difficult to let go of resentful feelings such as frustrations and anger from continuous exposure to manipulation, and this builds deep inside your system.

And finally, Stockholm syndrome can be triggered when the victim sympathizes with the manipulator and defends his or her way of thinking. The victims give in heartily to the fact that they need to be victims for the good of the manipulator. This is, perhaps, the deepest level of change in thinking and state of mind that a manipulator can cause.

Effects of Manipulation on the Manipulator

The effects of manipulation on victims is a well-known element in the equation, and most of us will agree that such effects are possible. Additionally, multiple scientific studies done by various authorized entities have proven the existence of the harmful effects of manipulation on the victims. Some of them have been discussed in the earlier section of this chapter. Now, it is time to discuss the manipulation from the manipulator perspective.

Why do people use manipulation? - All of us at some points in time, end up unwittingly or wittingly using manipulation to achieve our ends. Parents use it on their children in the name of parenting care, and partners use it on each other in the name of love, bosses use it on employees in the name of challenging them to bigger roles, and so forth. And moreover, it is not as if the manipulators don't feel the pain of using subversive tactics. Most of them also undergo the pain of using manipulation repeatedly to keep what they believe is 'happiness and love' in their lives. So, why do these people continue to use manipulation despite knowing about its harmful effects?

Also, it is important to remember that manipulation by itself is not a bad thing. Only when it gets uncontrollable, and people use manipulation as the primary and the only tool to achieve results, then it is a cause for concern. We are going to look at the manipulation of the second kind; the kind in which it is used to control the lives of other people. So, why do people get manipulative in their lives? Here are some reasons:

Manipulators are driven by a sense of fear, unworthiness, hopelessness, and helplessness - Manipulators hold a very deep fear that they will not get the desired outcomes from life without manipulation. This fear is grounded in their lack of self-worth and self-confidence. They feel so unworthy of themselves that they start to believe that the only way they can ever achieve their desired results is by manipulating and controlling other people to achieve their ends. Here is a small list of fears that manipulators with the lack of self-worth and self-confidence have:

- Fear of not getting what they want on their own merits

- Fear that life and the other people surrounding them will not favor them

- Fear that everything in their life is positioned against them

- Fear that they will not get what they want; but, others will get their desires fulfilled

- Fear of abandonment

- Fear that this is a 'dog-eat-dog' world with regard to emotions, money, and relationships

- Fear that resources are highly limited and nothing can be achieved without manipulation and control

Manipulators feel that they are not worthy of having good things happening to them. They feel they are unworthy of having joy and happiness. Consequently, they try to get these elements through manipulation and control. Therefore, the fears mentioned above are all based on one belief that they are not worthy.

Manipulators lack consciousness - Manipulators do not recognize or accept the fact that each of us is responsible for our own lives. Such people do not recognize the connection between their inner selves and external circumstances. They cannot correlate between the two. They don't realize that what is within us is what is represented or manifested in the outside world.

Manipulators disbelieve in the existence of this connection so deeply that they refuse to learn from their repeated mistakes and painful episodes from enduring manipulative behaviors that tell them the truth of connecting the internal and external worlds. It looks as if these people don't want to learn and evolve. They refuse to accept the truth that our actions and external manifestations are outcomes of our internal thoughts and beliefs.

This lack of consciousness makes manipulators perceive the world as 'unsafe.' Consequently, they think that using manipulation in this 'unsafe' world is the only way to get what they want even if it means pain, agony, and suffering that comes along with manipulative tactics. So, when they realize that one manipulation has achieved its end, then they automatically move onto the next manipulation. They keep moving from one manipulation to another because deep down they know that this kind of living will never give them an authentic life. They do it to hide their sense of unworthiness and the fear derived from this feeling.

The ultimate purpose of manipulation is to derive a sense of self-worth and to overcome this lack of consciousness and connection to the world.

Manipulators are low on self-esteem - There are two ways people handle low self-esteem. One is for them to become victims of unscrupulous manipulators, and another one is to become the manipulator themselves.

People with low levels of self-esteem are always looking for ways to build their facade of control. As they lack the necessary skills and the right kind of attitude to build the necessary skills to develop self-esteem, they turn to manipulation to achieve this end. Manipulating people weaker than themselves is, perhaps, the first and simplest way to build self-esteem, even if it is only as a facade to hide their own weaknesses and problems that go deeper than the surface. Such people use manipulation for self-enhancement and self-protection.

One of the most common forms of manipulation used by people with low self-esteem is to charm women into liking them. Once the women fall into the 'charm' trap, then the manipulators' real personality comes forward, and the process of controlling the hapless woman is complete.

What Goes On In the Minds of Manipulators?

Before that, do you know that manipulators can be helped out of their manipulative behaviors? Yes, they can be, and that is one of the primary reasons why we must learn to understand what goes on in their minds.

It is common to find a lot of information about how to identify manipulators, label them, and either ignore or judge them for what they are. While this is a good thing to keep innocent people from getting hurt, it is equally important for us to try and dig deeper into the minds of the manipulators and try to help them instead of outrightly painting them as the demons they are made out to be.

And yet, it is vital to remember that there is no need to condone or validate the actions of manipulators. Instead, it is only by learning to try to understand them better than they can be helped in facing up to and overcoming the challenges that lie deep in their psyche. So, what goes on in the minds of manipulators?

Manipulators and communication skills - First, most of the manipulators have a huge problem with their communication skills. We all learn how to communicate from the interactions we have with the people around us. We watch, observe, and ape the behavior and attitude of the influencers in our lives. So, if you choose a dysfunctional person to learn your communication skills, you are likely to pick up their dysfunctional habits without realizing your mistake.

In fact, most manipulators are puzzled by the fact that most people find their behavior and attitude strange. They are of the belief that they are doing things correctly, and that you are wrong. One of the main reasons why manipulators come off as authentic is because they deeply believe in their own reality. They just don't understand their way of behaving and communicating is different and that they have to change to adapt to the accepted ways of society.

Many manipulators have learned to ask for things in the wrong way. For example, they may have learned that saying yes is easier than saying no and prefer to do so, and then find ways to defend their stance through manipulation. Conversely, they find it difficult to interpret the responses of other people too. So, a 'yes' is misinterpreted as maybe or a 'no' as a 'yes.' This misunderstanding comes from their own learning from the wrong kinds of people.

They could have learned to say no to something when they actually want it, a strange behavior that evolved from being brought up by overly strict, or even abusive, parents. So, if you suspect that you are in a relationship with a manipulative person, then it might make sense for you first to accept that his or her 'yes' could just be a 'maybe.' This kind of forewarning regarding the uncertainty in the responses of manipulators helps you handle the relationship in a more productive and less harmful manner than before.

A manipulator could be telling you to leave him alone when he actually wants your company. When you do as he says, then he will get angry at you because you were not there for him. You see the conflicts going on in his mind. So, every level of manipulation entails a need, and if you can gauge that underlying need, you can choose to either fulfill it or find ways to deflect the situation effectively, causing little or no pain both for you and the manipulator.

Some psychological experts believe that the biggest problem with manipulators is that they have not evolved into adulthood and the accompanying behavioral changes. A manipulator is a small child who has refused to grow up. Sometimes, this refusal is unintentional because they believe they are doing the right thing because this is what was taught to them.

Therefore, most of us make the mistake of thinking that all acts of manipulators, including scheming, plotting, etc. are actually natural behavior from their perspective.

Goals of Manipulation

Regardless of the type of manipulation used, all manipulators want the same things from life as another average, normal human beings. Manipulators desire materialistic well-being, sex, strong relationships, and above all, want love and understanding from the people in their lives. The only difference between manipulators and normal people is that the former believe that manipulation is the only way they can get these desires. They think 'normal people' are actually abnormal.

A shift in perspective is all that is needed to bring manipulators to their senses, though it is easier said than done, especially if you are the victims bearing the brunt of their abominable behavior. Sadly, manipulators don't see the fact that manipulation only gets them hatred, ignorance, or worse still, pity.

Finally, imagine yourself in the position of the manipulator. Imagine a world in which you are trying to say 'yes' in your language, and the entire universe is reading it as 'no.' Imagine being misunderstood at every stage of your life, and it has so often now that you feel detached from the world around you.

Gaslighting

On some rare occasions, you find someone who learns to love and understand you. Wouldn't you do everything you could to keep that person in your life? Does it not seem natural that this manipulator does not want to let go of the one breath of fresh air that he has been able to access in a world filled with people unwilling to listen or understand him? Well, that is what most manipulators go through, and maybe, sometimes, it is possible to help such people help themselves.

At this stage, it is important to repeat the fact this 'understanding' perspective towards manipulators does not condone or validate manipulative. It is only an attempt to try and understand the working of their minds so that we can help them overcome their problems, which is a good thing for the manipulators as well as the victims.

It is a pointer to a possible fact that the person whose manipulative control you are under could be hiding a highly vulnerable, hurt individual deep down, and you could help in bringing out that person who could have the power to love and show affection without malice. Manipulators are invariably cowards who try to hide their cowardice in an outward pretense of bravado. If you can teach such people that being scared is not a sign of weakness, then they are more willing to expose their hurt than before giving them the opportunity to get rid of old hurts and pains.

Failures Commonly Encountered by Manipulators

Although manipulators try to control other people through nasty and unpleasant means, they rarely get the satisfaction of being happy in their lives. Here are some common failures that nearly all manipulators encounter in their lives:

- They face numerous relationship and communication issues considering that they never learn to be honest and open with people.

- They get alienated from all the people whom they have cheated, harmed, or caused pain to in any way. Also, these stories go around in their social circle, and even those who were victimized by the manipulator keep away from him or her, thanks to the warnings given by earlier victims.

- Their professional and personal reputation takes a big hit, and they become known as unreliable, untrustworthy, and inauthentic.

- As they lose credibility, they end up losing a lot of good opportunities in their professional and personal lives.

- Manipulators also suffer from low self-esteem because deep down, they know they are 'frauds.' They can hardly be taken in by their own fakeness.

- They never have truly wholesome relationships considering their high levels of self-absorption and self-interest.

- The manipulator experiences physical, emotional, mental, and spiritual distress driven by shame and a guilty conscience.

- And finally, most manipulators struggle to live with themselves as they are continually going through internal moral and ethical conflicts.

Manipulators Can Change

The heartening thing about all human behaviors is that they can be changed. In the same vein, manipulators, especially the unintentional ones, can be taught to change for the positive. All they need is a facilitator, and someone who can help them find help better in this regard but their own victims (invariably loved ones who still care for them) who are likely to know the manipulators' personalities inside out, and they can reach out to professionals who can make a big difference.

Facilitators can help manipulators unlearn bad behavior and teach new behaviors that are acceptable to society. When you, a person who cares for and wants to help the manipulator, reaches deep down and touches his or her core being, then you are doing the person a big favor. Do it if you can. Before that, you must learn to understand the child within the manipulator, and his inability to break out from the shackles of thoughts and ideas carried forward from his childhood.

It is very important to remember that a manipulator can change for the positive only if he or she wants to. You cannot change them if they don't want to. That is a vital warning sign to look out for if you intend to help someone like this in your life. Moreover, remember that helping manipulators is not your obligation.

Gaslighting

CHAPTER 6

Standing Up For Yourself

While there is no doubt that the manipulators have their own set of problems to deal with, you as a victim have every right to stand up and fight for yourself in the face of intense and uncontrollable manipulation. Yes, you must try and help the manipulator too.

But, not before you have helped yourself to overcome the dark effects of sustained exposure to dangerous and harmful gaslighting and manipulative behaviors. Standing up for yourself is the first thing you do, and when you are free, then you can go back and help the manipulator solve his or her underlying problems. So, let's jump right in.

Before giving you certain tips for countering manipulative techniques specifically in certain situations like in romantic relationships, at the workplace, in the family, etc. let us look at some learning tips that help you build your ability to recognize and manage manipulation in your life. These tips, when mastered, will help you handle manipulation and stand up strongly for yourself.

Common Tips to Help Counter Manipulation

Build Self-Awareness

One of the most significant reasons for many of us to become a victim of manipulation is that we cannot identify with ourselves. We have little or no idea about what is going on in our lives. We don't know what we want and simply drift along without a purpose.

Then, someone walks into our life, and inexplicably we take on their purpose as ours. If the person genuinely cares for us, then he or she will help us understand ourselves better. However, if the person is looking for a victim to manipulate and control, then we get stuck in the mire. Here are some reasons as to why building self-awareness is a critical tool to avoid being gaslighted:

Self-awareness develops your emotional intelligence - The more aware you are of yourself, your emotions, and how you react to them, the easier it is for you to preempt negative situations and work out ways to either avoid them or fight them. With a well-developed emotional setup, it becomes easy to identify manipulators and signs of manipulative tactics. In fact, with repeated practice, the power of your gut instincts improve considerably helping you recognize negative vibes that you might be getting from pretending charmers.

Self-awareness builds consciousness - You can act consciously and take intentional and informed decisions regarding all aspects of your life. You will be able to look at everything happening in your life objectively and rationally empowering you to see things lying underneath the facades that people are putting up to fool you.

Interestingly, despite knowing the importance of self-awareness, most of us find it difficult to become self-aware. The reason for that is that we are not taught to be present 'in the moment' and observe everything around us and within us, objectively and without judgment. We are all trained to react and respond to situations quickly (as it is considered efficient to act quickly), and therefore, we end up doing things impulsively. We don't give ourselves time to observe and imbibe the events and feelings in our lives and end up living like an automaton.

In fact, manipulators are more self-aware than the average person on the street because he or she needs it to survive and thrive in the world through control and manipulation. Therefore, building self-awareness helps you counter manipulators in a better way than otherwise.

Tips to build self-awareness - So, how does one increase self-awareness? Here are some suggestions that you can use. Practice if you want to get the full benefits of self-awareness.

Create some space and time for yourself - Regardless of how busy you are, you must make it mandatory to find some space and time when you can be with no one but yourself. Keep away from devices and their interrupting notifications. Just start with five minutes each day, and do nothing but sit quietly and observe your thoughts. Don't react or respond to them. Simply watch your thoughts and follow them one at a time. You will notice that each thought increases intensity, reaches a peak, and slowly fades away to give way to the next thought, which goes through the same routine.

Every thought brings feelings too. Connect with the emotions of each thought. If your mind is on last year's family holiday, you could feel happy remembering it. Again, don't react. Simply watch your emotions, which also follow the path of the thought. They increase in intensity in proportion to the thought and ebb away as the thought fades.

Do this exercise on a daily basis. Initially, it is going to be frustrating because our thoughts are quite random. However, if you focus and practice every day, you will find it increasingly easy to hold a thought and stay with it until it fades away into oblivion.

Practice mindfulness - Mindfulness is the art of being 'at the moment' fully and completely engaged with your current activity. Mindfulness calls for complete immersion in the task you are doing. Do you think you are mindful? Here is an example of telling you that mindfulness has to be practiced and does not come naturally until you make it a habit in your life.

Suppose you are peeling potatoes. What happens? Your hands are busy peeling potatoes. Your mind is somewhere else lost in some random thoughts, or even, on one thing that is central to your life at that moment in time. Your mind is totally disconnected from your physical self, which is caught up in peeling potatoes. This is the opposite of mindfulness.

Here is what mindfulness will be like in the same situation. Your hands are peeling potatoes, and your mind is also following the movement of your hands in the peeling action. You are aware of how you are standing or sitting while you are peeling the potatoes. You can feel the stress of standing in the same position for a long time, and yet, you continue to peel potatoes.

You know that when you pick up a potato, you are breathing in, and when you are putting down the peeled potato, you are breathing out. It could be the reverse for you. The thing is that you are aware of how you are breathing even as you peel potatoes. You know exactly how many potatoes you have peeled until now, and how many more are left over. You are not working in an automatic mode but are keenly conscious of every element of the action associated with peeling potatoes.

So, being mindfulness is putting your body, heart, and mind into the current task. When you do this, you feel focused and do not lose out to distractions around you. You not only increase your productivity, but you find yourself feeling refreshed and energized at the end of the task.

Moreover, you are building your self-awareness through mindfulness. You are not caught up with idle thoughts that create needless panic in your head. You are immersed and completely engaged in peeling potatoes, and you enjoy every moment of your life.

So, practice mindfulness in every action of your life, and build self-awareness even as you find the power to discern between useful and useless thoughts and emotions that come to disrupt your life. Knowledge is power, and with this power, you can keep manipulators at bay.

Keep a journal - Writing down your thoughts is one of the best ways to know what you are thinking and feeling. In a manipulative state, the more you write down your ideas and beliefs, the easier it gets to differentiate between imagination and reality. This power to differentiate gives you the strength to handle manipulation and use measures to counter it.

Build Self-Confidence

What is self-confidence? It is the ability to know your strengths and weaknesses with regard to the environment you are in so that you can leverage the advantages available to you at that point in time. Self-confidence is founded on self-belief, where you believe in your strength to do the things that are best for you. So, the more self-confident you are, the less likely you will be to fall prey to a manipulator's whims. Here are some recommendations you can use to build self-confidence:

Visualize yourself as being confident - Your mind is a powerful tool that can help you achieve your dreams. When you visualize yourself as being confident and strong, then your subconscious mind drives your body to achieve what you have dreamed. Low confidence is rooted in our belief that we are worthless and useless. Change this idea in your mind and gather the courage to convert it into reality.

Use confidence-building affirmations - Affirmations are excellent to 'install' thoughts into your heart and mind. When you say you are no good, then you begin to believe in your words. When you repeatedly say that you are good enough for yourself, then you begin to believe in these words. Therefore, use positive words about your self-image and repeat them as often as you can. Here are a few examples:

- I am confident and strong.
- I am capable.
- I am worthy of love and happiness.

Every day, do one thing that scares you - Fear plays a vital part in denting our confidence. A great way to overcome fear is to face it regularly so that you learn to deal with it. So, take one thing you are scared of doing, and do it at least once every day. For example, if you lack the courage to speak to strangers, make it a point to speak to one stranger a day. You don't have to start a conversation. A simple hello or even pretending to ask for directions is fine. The trick is to face the fear that comes with the act of talking to strangers. The more you do it, the more you will realize that your fear is unfounded, and it will become easy to overcome it.

Face your inner critic - We all have a voice in our head that keeps telling us that we should not get out of our comfort zone because we are not good enough. Face this critic in your head and argue your point fearlessly. Talk to it about the many strengths you have, and if need be, simply silence it.

Learn to accept rejections - Being rejected, failing, etc. are all part of human life. We cannot escape from it. And yet, we are so scared of rejections and failures that we don't want to try anything new. This kind of 'safe' attitude becomes an easy target for manipulators. They know that people who are scared of failures will do anything to prevent trying to get out of their comfort zones. Manipulators will use this against hapless people.

So, learn to face failures by accepting the fact that they come in your life to make you stronger than before. Manipulators will rarely seek out confident and strong people.

Enhance Your Friends' Circle

Human beings are social animals, and we need people to talk to and communicate with to survive. In times of need, it is people we reach out to, right? The larger your circle of friends, the more people you can seek help from. When you are under the mercy of a manipulator, you need multiple perspectives so that you can opt for the optimal solution. And for this, you need a lot of people who can give you numerous perspectives.

Additionally, a large circle of friends is a great deterrent to manipulators because they prefer to work on lonely people. Here are more advantages to having a healthy number of friends in your life:

- It gives you new and innovative perspectives on life and experiences.

- It helps you see both positives and negatives in any given solution, which, in turn, facilitates making informed choices.

- It helps you get out of your comfort zone, and consequently, build your self-confidence.

- It improves your knowledge levels and skills as people from varied backgrounds are likely to share their experiences and knowledge with you.

Take Time-Outs Regularly

If you don't take regular breaks from your hectic pace of life, you are likely to be filled with resentment which, in turn, will lead you to become depressed, anxious, and unhappy; a perfect target for manipulators. You must always strive to be happy and to do that; you must find ways to unwind regularly.

Do the things you love during these breaks. Stay away from electronic devices that keep disturbing you. Connect with yourself when you take your breaks. You will return refreshed and rejuvenated ready to take on the challenges of the world. Breaks give you the opportunity to reflect on your life and find gaps that need filling up.

Reach Out for Help

It is almost impossible to live alone in this world. Being social animals, we constantly need to connect with other people, which not only keep you happy and energized but also help to get a different perspective of your life. Additionally, there are people out there who are capable of helping you out in times of need. All that is needed is to ask for help. Don't hesitate to do so.

Seeking help when in trouble is the wisest thing you can do because being a victim of manipulation can take its toll on your ability to think straight, and you need a professional or a trusted person to help you see things in the right perspective.

Manipulation Countering Techniques in Relationships

Other than the above common elements that help in building a strong character, here are some tips that will help you manage manipulation in different aspects of your life. This section deals with manipulation counter techniques in relationships, at the workplace, and in the family. So, let's start with relationships.

Here are a few pointers to recall and summarize the tell-tale signs of being the victim in a manipulative relationship:

Your partner shifts between Dr. Jekyll and Mr. (or Ms.) Hyde - Manipulative partners typically have two faces; one of the soft-hearted, kind, and caring Dr. Jekyll, and another of the monstrous and controlling Mr. (or Ms. Hyde). If your partner is shifting between these two personalities, then he or she could be the manipulative partner.

Your partner presents passive-aggressive behaviors - They use underhanded means to hurt you. They are jealous of every other relationship you have in life, including those with your siblings and parents. They show you the silent treatment more often than you can handle. Such is a manipulative partner.

Your relationship could be stressing you out - Do you feel stressed whenever you spend time with your partner? If yes, then beware of manipulation and the effects it is having on your life. So, if any of the above signs exist in your life, then what can you do to help yourself? Here are a few suggestions:

Look at your relationship rationally - Be rational and get a good look at where and how your relationship is panning out. Take a pen and paper and write down notes. Recall the times when you felt happy with your partner, and delve deep into your mind, and see if you can pinpoint the time when the relationship began to sour. Leave out the emotions from your observation points. Read what you have written, and if you don't like it, then there is a problem.

Set clear boundaries and reiterate them as often as you can - Discuss with your partner and let him or her know where the line separating acceptable and unacceptable elements are drawn. Don't leave out opportunities to remind yourself and your partner about these boundaries.

Don't hold yourself responsible for your partner's behavior - Your partner cannot find an excuse and blame you for his or her bad behavior. Be firm and make sure your partner takes responsibility for his or her behavior and actions.

Do not accept any excuses for bad behavior - Bad behavior has to be kept in check, and no excuse regardless of how authentic it might seem should be used to substantiate the behavior. Right from the beginning, make sure you don't miss opportunities to correct irrational behavior of your partner without fear.

Take responsibility for your behavior too - Stand your ground and be prepared to accept the outcome of your own behavior. Suppose you ticked off your partner for something nasty he or she did, and you are likely to lose the relationship, then so be it. Prepare yourself to move on. The fear of losing out on things is one of the primary causes of becoming a victim to manipulation.

Reach out for help - Your partner's friends, family or your own friends and family are all standing by to help you. Learn to trust other people too, and reach out for help when you know that things are turning unpleasant. Asking for help is not a sign of weakness. It is a sign of strength and courage. An outside perspective is almost always unbiased, and therefore, seeking help from the people around you is also a way of helping you look at things objectively and rationally.

Let your partner know that the relationship is causing you pain and you are looking for a change - If things are not going well for you, then don't waste time sending clear messages to your partner that you are undergoing pain and are keen on seeing positive changes, failing which you are ready to face the consequences of a fallout.

And finally, if all else fails, do not hesitate to get out of the relationship. Nothing is more important than your life. In fact, if kids are involved in a relationship, you might have to take a stern decision sooner and faster than in the absence of kids.

No one deserves a stressful relationship, and yes, while the consequences of a failed relationship can be heartbreakingly painful, it is still better than to remain in the toxicity and live in lifelong agony. So, stand up for yourself, belief in the fact that you deserve better, and get a hold on your life.

Manipulation Countering Techniques at the Workplace

There are many ways you can counter manipulation techniques in your office; some of them are intense and some simplistic ones to manage your day-to-day problems arising out of manipulation at the workplace. Manipulation at the workplace usually takes place in disguised ways so that you think that they are working in your interests. In reality, these manipulators will have only their interests in mind, and everyone else can jump into a well, for all they care.

For example, they will act concerned, and tell you that everyone in the office thinks that you are useless and unworthy. They will say they want to help you change the way the office people look at and treat you. They will say they will teach you how to behave, improve your attitude, and much more. They will veil their threat to control you by saying that if you don't follow their ideas, your professional life will be ruined. This is what manipulators in the workplace want you to believe.

In truth, they don't care what happens to you. They want to control you so that they can validate their lives and use you to achieve their ends while you prevent yourself from growing and expanding your professional horizons. It is better to be wary of such individuals and not allow them to enter into your life because once they get control of you, then they will make false promises, slip away or hit back at you if you try to hold them accountable, and simply make your life miserable.

Ignore manipulators - Ignoring manipulators is one of the best ways to put them off in the first place. Moreover, studies have shown that ignoring offensive people and manipulators actually enhance your productivity and intelligence. The more you give in to the manipulator's gaslighting tactics, the more you will waste away your mind space and productivity.

If you choose to correct manipulators, you will only fall deeper into the trap, and getting out will get increasingly difficult. Therefore, ignoring manipulators at the workplace is a great way to counter their efforts to control you. Silence is truly golden in such circumstances.

However, it is not always possible to ignore and keep yourself safe from manipulative marauders. You must use more intense tactics to counter them. Here are a few of them to help you lead a more productive and manipulation-free life at your workplace.

Get offensive if you need to - Manipulators are continually finding ways to destabilize you. Sometimes, you can ignore them. But, sometimes, you cannot. In such situations, it is best to get on the offensive and destabilize them. Find what gives them the support needed to manipulate you. It could be a senior manager, a friend, or even a wily subordinate. Take your offensive to them and show them your professional tenacity. In the absence of any support, manipulators can back off.

Trust your judgment - Remember that no one knows your life purposes better than you. Don't depend on other people to define who you are or what you do. Taking feedback for self-improvement is good. However, don't take feedback so seriously that you alter your personality because you think you are not good enough to achieve your dreams.

Trust and define yourself based on your own experiences and belief system. When you stand strong on your own foundations, then the chances of falling for manipulators' traps are reduced drastically.

Don't try to fit into other people's lives - Many times, in our efforts to fit into the surrounding environment, we chose not to try new things. Avoid falling into this trap. Keep reinventing yourself, and find ways to indulge in new experiences and learning. The trick here is that most manipulators at the workplace use your sense of consistency to push their own agenda.

For example, a manipulative boss will demand punctuality from you while he or she chooses to come in late to work. And you will be manipulated into doing your boss's work instead of finishing up your own tasks so that you can leave early. To avoid this kind of a situation, it is best for you to keep reinventing yourself so that you can find a lot of opportunities outside the influence of this manipulative boss.

Moreover, your consistency and the lack of innovative attitude will help manipulative people box you into nothingness, leaving you little or no room for improvement. Push your learning and working boundaries and do your work in a way that makes you stand out, and people other than the manipulator will notice you and offer you new positions and responsibilities.

Don't compromise on your principles - Using guilt is a powerful tool that manipulators use to control you. Manipulators will continually remind you of your past mistakes and failures in an effort to dent your confidence and happiness. Manipulators are of the opinion that people should not be happy and satisfied, and this belief is rooted in their own unhappiness and lack of achievements.

When manipulators keep reminding you of your mistakes and failures, they are effectively working at enhancing your self-doubt. You slowly begin to doubt your abilities and sense of self-worth. One of the primary powers of manipulators is based on your level of uncertainty. The more uncertain you are, the more control they have over you and your activities. Therefore, stop doubting yourself and feeling guilty about past mistakes. Learn valuable lessons from your mistakes and failures and move on.

Don't always wait for permission - When there is no intention to make mistakes or errors from your end, you don't have to really ask for permission to do some things. Remember that it is easier to say sorry than to wait in line and ask for permission to initiate things.

Be confident and do what you want to do, and don't end up wasting your time waiting for permission for people. Unlearn what we as humans have been taught; that we have to wait in line to talk. No, many times, the line will not move. So, you make a move and say and do what you want to do, provided you know that you have no 'malicious' intent in your heart and mind.

In fact, manipulators use this 'asking for permission' against us. They tell us that if we keep quiet in meetings, then we will get a promotion by the end of the year. This makes us feel scared to raise our voices to explain our new and innovative ideas or even raise our hands to give an opinion. Manipulators talk of some vague rules regarding politeness and courtesy to prevent us from voicing our fears and concerns.

So, don't wait for permission. By doing so, you are only falling into the trap of control that manipulators are laying for you.

Take control of your professional life - Remember your life is your own, and no one can make it better or worse but you. This holds good for your career too. It is entirely up to you to take control of your professional life and take strides in your career that will help you achieve your goals and life purposes. The choice to take control is in your hands. Find the answer to the following question: Do I want to lead my life my way or the way of someone else?

Also, take responsibility for your career. Don't blame it on others around you. If your career is not taking off and you are constantly in a state of stagnation, then you are as responsible for the state as your manipulator, perhaps, more so, considering that you are the driver of your life. It is not only naive but also an escapist attitude if you just float around in your life, finding multiple people to blame for your mistakes and failures. Stop complaining, take responsibility, and get ahead.

Find your purpose in life - One of the main reasons why manipulators are able to manipulate others is because most of us have no idea what our life purpose is. What do you want to achieve in your career? What are your professional goals? In the absence of these gaps in self-awareness, manipulators are able to sow the seeds of their own goals and purposes and use you to achieve their desired results. When you feel out of control, take a day off, sit quietly in your room, and reflect on the purpose of your career. What do you want to do in your profession, and why?

Once these questions are answered, then the how to achieve the purpose falls into place automatically. Manipulators are left with no room in your heart and mind space to put in their ideas and thoughts.

Take time to reflect on your work and on yourself regularly. If you are continuously busy and have no time for your heart and mind, then too, manipulators will find their gaps and get into your life. The lack of time spent with yourself leads you to distraction because you tend to lose focus on things. Moving from one task to another, and then to a third leaves you with no time and energy to focus on yourself. The more distracted you are in life, the easier it is to fall into the trap of manipulation.

And finally, remember that no one can manipulate you without your permission. Take accountability for your life events and do the things you need to do to turn around your profession.

Manipulation Countering Techniques in the Family

When it comes to dealing with manipulative partners, bosses, and coworkers, at least you know that they are not family, and can bring in a little bit of objectivity in your interactions with them. Dealing with manipulators within a family is far, far more stressful than this. Family members are the ones we trust the most, right? And if such people manipulate you for their ends, then it is almost as if you lose trust in the world. Well, sadly, gaslighting happens in family environments too, and it is imperative that you stand up and fight for yourself before it is too late.

Identify other victims of the manipulative family member - In a family setup, manipulators are likely to have more than one victim. For example, if one of the parents is the manipulator, then the victims would be all the children, and maybe even the spouse. Get the victims together and discuss concerns in a group.

Focus on your state of mind - What is going on in your head? Are you doing things you want to do or are you blindly following the manipulator's lead? Get objective with your life and think for yourself. Learn to be independent and build the necessary skills for it.

Set clear boundaries - Once you are clear that you are being manipulated, start acting immediately. First, set clear boundaries with your manipulator. These boundaries are better managed if they are physical in nature. For example, if you have a separate room at home, then get yourself a new set of locks for your door, and keep it locked always. Don't give the key to anyone else, including the people you trust because they could also be victims of the same manipulator who could use this trusted person to get your room keys.

Identify intangible boundaries and areas where the manipulator is influencing your thoughts. Ensure you stay clear away from these areas so that you minimize contact with him or her. Also, engage with the manipulator only in a safe and open environment. Avoid staying alone with him or her. If you have no choice but to be alone, then make sure you put as much distance as you can between you and him or her.

Manipulation Countering Techniques When Dealing with Adult Children

Victimized parents can use the following suggestions and recommendations when dealing with manipulative adult children. The trick in this situation is that you are dealing with your child, and subjectivity comes into play far more than you can imagine as compared to other situations. So, beware of this element and be calm during your interactions with your child. However, don't be scared of displaying a firm attitude as you set forth the following guiding principles on which you expect your child to behave.

Set clear time limits - Let your child know how long you intend to help him or her. Let your child know that he or she has to find his own ways of dealing with life problems. Ask gently probing questions like what are your plans? By when do you hope to get out of this issue?

If your child comes back with some evasive answer, then offer solutions from your end, and take the discussion forward. End such conversations with confidence-building statements like, 'I believe in your capabilities and resourcefulness to solve your own problems. You will feel better if you spend some time and effort on the issue and write down your thoughts and solutions that come to your mind. I am sure you will come up with something good.'

Don't hesitate to tick off your child if you see excessive use of guilt-ridden manipulation - It is very easy to feel guilty when your child reminds you of past mistakes and failures and uses them against you today. While there may be some truth in what the child says, he or she has no right to hold you to ransom now. In fact, there could be numerous other ways in which you have already paid for and left behind those errors. So, if your child is repeatedly trying to get you on a guilt-trip, then stand your ground and don't hesitate to tick them off. Don't allow yourself to be manipulated by people who showed ideally show gratitude for many things you have done for them.

Encourage (you might have to insist on some cases) your working child to contribute to his or her room and boarding expenses - And there is nothing wrong with this attitude. The child is an adult who has to anyway take care of himself or herself. If the child is living with you for whatever reason, then he or she must not back away from contributing to the family expenses. Although this might come across as cruel, it works well to set clear boundaries between you and your adult children. The boundaries offer excellent protection from manipulative tactics of your adult child.

And if your adult child is yet to find gainful employment, make sure he or she helps out in the household chores like cleaning, cooking, gardening, etc. Not only are you setting boundaries with this attitude but also helping your child learn something useful. Don't think this approach represents a cruel attitude.

Control the money you dole out to your adult children - Don't give out money as and when they ask for it. Ask plenty of questions, put up blockages, give other options like taking a loan or waiting until they begin to earn before having desires to go on spending sprees, etc. Make sure you dole out money to adult children in proportion to their efforts in finding gainful employment.

Beware of getting caught off-guard - Manipulative adult children commonly try and catch their parents when they are off-guard to get their desires fulfilled. For example, you could suddenly get a message from your son with the money, 'I need money.' It is natural to feel scared that something bad has happened and you immediately and impulsively send the required amount. Now, remember to be wary of such off-guard requests.

Be prepared to answer without committing yourself to anything. For example, you could say, 'I don't know. I'll have to ask your mother (or father).' Alternately, you could say, 'I need more time. Let me see what I can do. I will get back to you by tomorrow afternoon' Take some time from your child, which will allow you to discuss some more and think and reconsider your decision if needed. Remember that manipulative people love to prey on people who act impulsively. Therefore, hold back your impulsive nature, or at least be wary of it.

Don't hesitate to change your mind - Yes, you did agree to something your child said. However, you are not obligated to follow through. You have every right to change your mind and not help out as you promised. Remember, the child is an adult, and his or her responsibilities are not yours. You have done what you could. Don't ruin your life (and that of your spouse or partner) by handing it over to the manipulations of irresponsible adult children. You are not in any popularity contest, and there is nothing left to prove to your child or to the world, at least in this regard.

Countering manipulative measure is not just difficult but also high energy and time-sapping. You have to be on your guard continually to prevent yourself from falling prey to expert manipulators because they always find a way to achieve their ends. So, if after a certain point in time, you feel tired, do not hesitate to ask for help from others, including professionals in the counseling field.

Yet, during your attempts to salvage a relationship, try and be the bigger person in the picture even if you are the child. Remember that the manipulator has a mind of his or her own, and needs some help to unlearn the wrong things. And yet, always remember that your safety comes first. It is all about balance.

Again, it is time to reiterate that the minute you think there could be in danger if you continued to live with the concerned person, don't hesitate to even report to the concerned regulatory authorities. Empower yourself using all of the above suggestions so that you are ready to face the challenges of being in a manipulative relationship. Stand strong and fight back with all your might. Sometimes, remember you might need to help the manipulator to help yourself. However, when you know that nothing is working, and things continue to be in the same horrible state or things just get worse, then it is time to get out and run for your life.

CHAPTER 7

Path to Recovery

So, now you have managed to escape from the clutches of a manipulator, it is time to recover and heal yourself and find a better life for yourself. It is imperative that you don't turn bitter after that nasty episode of manipulation. Remember, bitterness makes your life more difficult than it should be. Therefore, take an oath to heal yourself and recover from the trauma and become the positive person you once were.

How to Spot Manipulative Behavior and Stay Safe in the Future

Most manipulators have the following four characteristics that set them apart from normal, average human beings. Learn to identify and recognize them so that you can stay away as far away from such people as you can.

- Manipulators are highly skilled at detecting your weaknesses.

- When they find your weakness, they use it against you.

- They will then use one or many of the multiple methods described in the book to convince you to sacrifice a part of yourself so that they can use you to serve their ends.

- Regardless of the setting (whether at home, in a relationship, or at the workplace), once the manipulator has trapped you, then he or she will not stop manipulating you unless you choose to put a stop on it.

Here are some uncompromising principles you must adopt to prevent yourself from falling prey to manipulative tactics again.

Know and stand up for your fundamental human rights - Make sure the following human rights are uncompromised in any of the new relationships that you plan to get into:

- You have the right to expect respectful treatment from everyone.

- You have the right to express your opinions, feelings, and desires, and these can be different from those of others.

- You have the right to set your own priorities and are not obliged to follow those of anyone else.

- You can say 'no' without feeling guilty.

- You have the right to get what you paid for.

- You have the right to do everything in your power to protect yourself against emotional, mental, and physical harm.

You must build a new relationship on the basis of these fundamental human rights only. They also represent your boundaries beyond which no one is allowed to enter without your permission.

Maintain a dignified distance - Most manipulators have a way of dealing with different people differently. With some, they are highly polite and courteous, and with a few others, they are nasty and unpleasant. They can take on a groveling attitude with some people too. The shift in personalities is starkly discernible in manipulators. If you do see such a scene, remember to maintain a dignified distance from this person.

Stop blaming yourself for everything - When you are free from the clutches of your manipulator, look back at your own behavior and make necessary changes for positive outcomes. If you have been trained into taking blame and accountability for all the wrong things that happened in your relationship, then unlearn the lesson.

You are not accountable for anyone but yourself. Don't feel guilty and blame yourself for everything. If things go wrong in a new relationship, look at it objectively and find what can be corrected. Don't go about taking responsibility for the other person's behavior and attitudes. Ask yourself the following questions:

- Am I getting treated with respect?

- Are expectations being kept at reasonable levels?

- Is the relationship favoring only one person or are both being benefited?

- Most importantly, are you feeling good in the relationship?

The answers to these questions are critical pointers towards whether the relationship is worth your effort or not. Don't hesitate to step back if you are feeling uncomfortable. Don't allow yourself to fall too deeply in new relationships.

Ask a lot of questions and don't feel bad about it - An important reason you became a victim of manipulation earlier is that your questions were brushed under the carpet or you were made to feel silly for asking them. Don't repeat that mistake. Make sure you ask probing questions, and if you don't get satisfactory answers, maybe you must raise your radar.

Take time to respond to requests and queries - Most manipulators will want responses and reactions almost immediately leaving you very little time to think things through. This situation suits the manipulator because he or she does not want you to think independently.

Remember this lesson, and always take time to respond or react. Go home, reflect on what is being asked, see if there are options better suited to your needs, and then revert to the person. If the individual pushes you needlessly, step back, and don't give in. You have succeeded in avoiding falling into the manipulation trap.

Beware of the following terms and phrases that are deeply connected to gaslighting and manipulation tactics:

Monitoring - This phrase is a warning sign specifically in romantic relationships. In the initial stages of any romantic relationship, it is normal to wonder and know what your partner is doing all the time. However, if your boyfriend or girlfriend is monitoring you and your whereabouts excessively, then you should treat it as a warning sign and pay closer attention to the person's behavior before committing yourself.

Object Constancy - When normal people are angry at someone, they don't forget the love and affection they still feel for the other person. However, gaslighters and narcissists turn off all the positive feelings they had for the victim and the insults and abuses hurled can hurt the very core of your being. This phenomenon, called object constancy, is the reason why manipulators appear to have starkly different personalities at different times.

People with this problem tend to see things that don't really exist and believe things that are not true. In their minds, these things and beliefs exist, and then they go berserk when you try to counter their ideas. They can get highly violent and use multiple controlling methods to manipulate and control you so that their truth remains unchanged. Beware of people who exhibit this kind of behavior.

Attraction to your skills - While some manipulators prey on people weaker than themselves, there is a rare breed of manipulators who are attracted to you because you are highly skilled and stand out from the ordinary crowd. You are likely to encounter such people in the workplace.

Your co-workers or even your bosses want to manipulate and control you because they want to show that you are not as good as them. So, if you feel your skills and strengths are continually being faulted, then you could be dealing with this kind of a manipulator.

Beware of liars - Manipulators are excellent liars and can flip the script to suit their needs. If you have already been a victim once, it will be very easy to identify lies told by manipulators. If and when you encounter people who lie and try to alter what they meant, you know you have to be on your guard.

Trauma bonding - If you were to look back on your period as a victim to a malicious manipulator, you would have wondered how you managed to stay in such a toxic environment and what made you stick to him despite being aware of the danger. The answer lies in trauma bonding.

Manipulators are not always cruel. They choose suitable and convenient events and times when they will shower praise and love on their victim for a while. During this time, the victim feels deeply attached to his or her manipulator. When the situation changes for the worse, and the cruelty begins again, the victim yearns for that love.

Manipulators manage to keep their victims on tender hooks alternating between short periods of bonding and affection and long periods of manipulation and control. The poor, hapless victim gets so accustomed to this push and pulls that he or she forgets to get out, and instead, works towards getting more of the short periods of love and affection. This is called trauma bonding.

Remember that abuse need not be in the physical form - Manipulators need not use physical abuse to manipulate you. In fact, most of them prefer to use emotional abuse to control their victims. So, don't get into a complacent mode if you think that you cannot find fault with the manipulator because he or she has not physically hit you or caused you harm. Emotional abuse is one of the most powerful forms of gaslighting techniques.

Bargaining their way through your life is a common tactic - When you threaten to leave the relationship, does your manipulator bargain with you and beg you to give him or her another chance? If it happens more than once, then you know you are dealing with a manipulator. Run from the person.

Don't forget to use the lessons you learned in the past to confirm and correct any potential mistakes you could repeat in the future. The traumatic pain of being in a manipulative relationship will, hopefully, be a thing of the past. However, don't forget the critical lessons learned.

How to Trust Yourself Again

An element that feels the impact of manipulation significantly is your intuition. After a bout of manipulative episodes, you are quite likely to lose trust in yourself. You find it exceedingly difficult to trust your instincts and treat everything and everyone around you with suspicion. In fact, the reasons why a manipulator was able to control you and your reality are:

- You were far too trusting and open than was good for you.

- The manipulator was successful in making you lose your trust in your gut instinct.

- He or she made you lose faith in your intuitive powers.

The manipulator was cunning and had got you tight in his or her hold. You are simply grateful for being out of the manipulator's clutches. All other good things, including learning to trust yourself, is put on the backburner. However, you must begin the process of trusting yourself and your intuition if you want to heal fully. Here are some pointers to get you going.

Remember that you never lost your intuition. Our intuitive powers are embedded in our psyche and can never be lost. It could have been muted or stilled for a while, thanks to the wily efforts of manipulators. But, you will never lose them. Therefore, take heart from this truth and work on recovering its power.

Start by going through how you are feeling presently. Are you happy, sad, depressed, or anxious? Then, ask yourself why you are feeling all these emotions. Think of a person and see if you can recognize your feelings for him or her. Do you enjoy thinking of the person, or do you think it is better to move on from thinking about the concerned individual?

Think of a food item and observe your feelings and thoughts about it. Are you salivating or feeling revulsion? If the feelings are vague or unclear, think of something else and repeat the exercise. In this way, you slowly start connecting with your intuition and setting the environment for its recovery.

Learning to trust yourself is going to take time. Your entire being has been assaulted multiple times and repeatedly. So, don't expect the ability to trust yourself come back to you overnight. It is a slow and hard process of self-healing. But, it will happen provided you don't hamper the process needlessly. Each time you find yourself being frustrated, tell yourself to be patient.

Breaking the bonds of trauma has to happen one at a time. Any activity or even a simple thought in your mind is likely to bring back horrific memories of the traumatic period. You must tackle each task with grit and determination until each painful memory is erased, or least soothed, in your mind. Repeat the process until you resemble your old self, the person you were before the manipulator came into your life.

And tell yourself this; if you can overcome this challenge in your life, you will be able to do anything else, and your future life is bound to be happy and joyful. So, until that time, hibernate into yourself and find ways to reconnect with your soul and become whole again. Take steps to cover up gaps that were created by the manipulator. Conserve your energy to be used for productive purposes only.

How to Prevent Yourself from Becoming Bitter and Begin the Healing Process

After a traumatic period of being under the control of ruthless, manipulative tactics, it is natural to feel bitter about everything in your life; the people, experiences, etc. In the initial periods after the break-off from the manipulator, you are likely to feel anger. Despite the negativity surrounding the feeling of anger, it can be a good thing because it can drive you to action so that you can make the best of whatever is left.

Bitterness is worse than anger because it leads you to a sense of utter helplessness. Bitterness comes from the belief that even anger is of no use because there is nothing left to do. Bitterness is something that leads to helpless inaction, which, in turn, could lead to a feeling of utter desolation and loneliness.

When you go through such deep emotion, remember one thing. Yes, you cannot undo what your manipulative partner, coworker, or family friend did to you. You cannot get back the lost time and energy. However, you can do a lot to put these bad experiences behind and move on with your life.

Bitterness and sustained resentment can lead to multiple problems including sleeplessness, loss of libido, and fatigue in the short term, and build-up of negative personality traits, low self-confidence, and a loss of purpose in the long term. While you can blame your manipulator for the problems created during the difficult times of being under his or her control, carrying forward the bitterness into your future life can be no one's fault but yours. Therefore, it is imperative that you make all efforts to let of the bitterness caused by the trauma of being in a manipulative relationship.

Re-evaluate your state of mind rationally - Sympathy from the people around us helps bitterness thrive in our lives. We keep repeating our story of trauma and agony to others, and thanks to their feelings of sympathy towards you, your bitterness continues to grow and expand. You begin to think that feeling bitter is your birthright and find comfort in it.

So, the first step to moving out of this comfort zone that you have found yourself is to do a serious re-evaluation of your status. Yes, you have gone through the trauma that few people would have had to bear. Yet, remember it is in the past, and holding on to the painful memories is only going to make your present and future horrible.

Dig deeper into your psyche and recall moments that you could have done better to prevent the condition. In such a case, aren't you partly responsible for what happened? What happened to make you so bitter? Are you feeling stupid for falling for the scam? Find the true answer within yourself. Take responsibility for the things you can. Use this lesson to wake up from your reverie and learn to let go of the past, including your mistakes and those of the perpetrator.

Stop telling your story of trauma to everyone - Put your story on hold. It is going to be difficult not to share your story with people, especially since you are not fully healed. But you can make a start. Begin by putting your story on hold for just one day. No matter who you meet on the chosen day, don't talk about your story. You will see that at the end of the day, even though some bit of emptiness from not sharing your story could be there, mostly there is an enormous relief, which comes from the fact that your mind did not feel compelled to feel sad today.

Push your boundaries and extend one day to two days to three days, and sooner than later, you will realize that even for you, the story has lost its charm. Consequently, sympathy will cease to flow, and your bitterness about life will slowly but surely begin to ebb.

Stop following your ex-manipulator - Thanks to the modern social media world, keeping track of people has become very easy. You are continually checking on the person's status updates, photos, social posts, etc. It is natural to follow the person who has created trauma in your life and see what he or she is up to. This natural need is based on the fact that you have not found the strength to let go.

The first thing you should do is to unfollow your ex-manipulator from every social media platform. Put the person out of all aspects of your life. Do this until you get back all the control over your life - completely and unequivocally. When your bitterness has died down, then you can go back and thank him (sarcastically, of course) for helping you learn valuable life lessons!

Face your hidden fears - After a traumatic experience, fearing a repeat of the same and failing to stand up yet again is a big deterrent to the healing process. You feel so scared of trying to get into new relationships that you simply write off your life, which, in turn, only enhances your bitterness to life. Moreover, bitterness feeds that fear of repeated failure.

The best way to handle this is to take your fear head-on, and when you do so, bitterness also gets reduced in your life. Take small baby steps towards building relationships. Start with a simple exercise like going out on a double-date with a trusted friend. Relearn your communication and relationship skills. When you find yourself making progress with these small steps, your fears will recede slowly, and so will your bitterness.

Forgive the manipulator - The power of forgiveness should not be underestimated. Forgive the manipulator; but, only when you are truly ready to forgive. Fake and forced forgiveness only enhances your resentment and anger. Here are some powerful reasons why you must prepare yourself to forgive:

- When you forgive, you realize that you have set a prisoner free, and slowly you will also realize that the prisoner was no one else but you. Holding on to forgiveness not only keeps the pain of anger and hurt alive but also kindles it.

- Stop thinking that you were wronged not because you were not wronged but because it will help you to forgive. Remind yourself that forgiving the manipulator will do nothing for him or her. But, it will heal your pain and hurt.

- Forgiving your perpetrator also includes forgiving yourself for the parts you have taken responsibility for.

- Forgiveness translates to letting go of hatred, which has the power to slowly eat you up and rot your heart and mind inside-out.

So, don't hold on to hurt, pain, and resentment. Forgive your manipulator and set yourself free, and get rid of bitterness from your life. It is important to reiterate here that does not forgive until you are truly ready to do so. Do it at your pace. But do it.

Learn to live 'in the now' - Bitterness refuses to leave your life because you are caught up in the past and living there. Wake yourself up and live in the present moment. Engage with the present experience you are going through. Bring your entire being, including your heart, mind, and body into the 'now.' There is no bitterness in the present moment, and this exercise will help you disconnect with this debilitating emotion.

Go out and try new experiences - Bitterness fades away in the presence of joy and excitement. So, go out and try new experiences. Indulge in a new hobby. Learn to sing, dance, paint, or play a new instrument. Rediscover an old passion and reconnect with it. Attend some kind of creative classes or anything else that you always wanted to, and bring in sunshine into your life.

Take one day at a time - Set little goals for yourself on a daily basis and try to achieve them. Don't work at more than a couple initially until you feel ready to take on a heavier load.

Take those baby steps towards getting rid of bitterness and welcoming back the sunshine in your life. You will see that it does not take very long for those baby steps to become huge strides of happiness and joy.

When to Seek Professional Help and Other Useful Resources

You have been trying hard on your own or with the help of your loved ones to reconnect with your old self and try and find ways to overcome the trauma of being in a manipulative experience. You have tried all there is to try, and yet you find yourself faltering. Now, it is time to seek professional help.

In fact, it might make sense to seek professional help earlier on itself whenever you felt that things are not really going right. There are multiple trusted counseling groups and professionals available who can help you find solutions to your problems. Additionally, do not hesitate to seek help for the manipulator too, especially if he or she is a loved one.

Also, there are multiple online forums and groups that you can join and share your experiences and learn from those of the others in the group. The more you seek help, the better are your chances to get out of the pain and agony of being a victim of manipulation.

The trick is recognizing and accepting that you and/or your manipulator needs help as soon as possible. Considering that your manipulator will not seek help, it might make sense, if you can, to help the other person too. But it is very important to remember that you come first. First, take care and protect yourself, and then do something for the manipulator, if you want. You are not obligated to help the manipulator even if he or she is a loved one. YOU COME, FIRST!

Thank you for reading my book...

Don't forget to leave an honest review...

I'd like to offer you this amazing resource which my clients pay for. It is a report I written when I first began my journey.

Click on the picture above or navigate to the website below to join my exclusive email list. Upon joining, you will receive this incredible report on how to recognize an abusive relationship.

Gaslighting

If you ask most people on the street what an abusive relationship is, chances are you'd get a description of physical abuse. And yes, that is most certainly an abusive relationship. However, abuse comes in many forms. The actual meaning of abuse is when someone exerts control over another person.

Find out more about recognizing an abusive relationship and learn how to take control over your life by clicking on the book above or by going to this link:

http://tinyurl.com/RecognizeAbusiveRelationship

CONCLUSION

So, summarily, the ideas, tips, and suggestions for recognizing and avoiding gaslighting can be briefly wrapped up.

Gaslighting is a form of manipulation that abusers use to control their victims. The most difficult aspect of identifying gaslighting behavior is that the manipulators skillfully and subtly convince their victims that they are going crazy. The victims believe that they are losing their sanity on their own. Victims get led to a distorted of reality.

Gaslighters are skilled at creating situations and taking advantage of vulnerabilities of victims to undermine them that seem innocuous to the innocent bystander. It takes a lot of practice and skill to identify gaslighting tactics.

Gaslighters use various techniques to achieve their end including withholding, countering, blocking or diverting, trivializing, denying or forgetting, and more to discredit the victims and make them feel that they are losing their minds.

Gaslighting can happen anywhere, including between parents and children, romantic partners, bosses and subordinates, and everywhere else where power dynamics come into play.

There are different kinds of manipulators and gaslighters, and each type uses different mechanisms depending on the need, state of mind of the victim, and other factors.

Manipulators use guilt, aggression, silent treatment, criticism, competition, attacking your self-esteem, and many more methods to control and manipulate you.

Ultimately, victims of gaslighting begin to doubt their own capabilities and realities and come completely under the influence of the manipulators to the extent that the latter control their minds.

Conclusion

Victims suffer from short-term and long-term effects of being in manipulative relationships. The effects on the victim range from sleeplessness, fatigue to chronic depression and even loss of sanity.

While victims feel a lot of pain and agony, manipulators also don't lead happy lives. They are also ridden by guilt, shame, alienation, and loss of love and affection right through their lives. They also need help, and it might make sense to help those who are genuinely looking to change their ways.

Telltale and warning signs of manipulators include:

- Lying and twisting facts
- Discernible shifting between two personality types
- Continually finding fault with you
- Withholding critical information and/or resources and the help of all kinds to weaken your stand
- Running away or blocking/diverting from discussing important topics
- Brushing your ideas and opinions under the carpet

Gaslighting

- Trivializing your thoughts, ideas, and your entire life

- Pretending things happened or didn't happen depending on the need

- Suddenly changing the subject

- Shifting blame for all the wrong things on you

- Isolating you from all your loved ones and friends

It is extremely important to stand up for yourself and fight against manipulators and gaslighters so that you can free yourself from their deadly clutches and lead your life on your terms.

Some important lessons you must master in order to stand up against manipulation include building self-awareness, developing confidence, expanding your social and friends circle, taking regular breaks for self-reflection, and reaching out for help when things go out of your control.

When you have been able to get out of the clutches of a manipulator, remember to get back on the recovery track as fast as possible. Learn not to allow the pain and agony of that traumatic experience to eat into your mind so much that you become irrevocably bitter in life.

Conclusion

Instead, find the strength to walk the difficult but happy path of recovery by allowing yourself to heal. Learn to forgive your manipulator because in doing so, you are letting go of the horrible past. Only when you let go can you move forward. Use the lessons learned to spot and stay away from manipulators in the future.

Learn to trust yourself and your intuitive powers. Your intuition is your faithful friend and will never leave you because it is deeply embedded in your psyche. While the trauma of manipulation might have dulled the power of your intuition, it will always be a part of you. Rediscover your ability to connect with your instincts and learn to live a good life.

Remember that no one can manipulate you unless you give them permission. Therefore, know what you want from life and make sure no one else decides how to lead your life. You are the master of your destiny.

And finally, there is plenty of help available to you in the form of family, friends, support groups, and professional counselors. Do not hesitate to reach out and seek help. Remember you are not alone in this fight against gaslighting. So, go and find help and get your life back under your control.

Gaslighting

Resources

http://gorovr.com/expanding-social-circle-can-positively-impact-life/

https://blog.melanietoniaevans.com/why-do-people-manipulate/

https://exploringyourmind.com/7-ways-identify-master-manipulator/

https://gaslightingbully.wordpress.com/tag/withholding/

https://journals.sagepub.com/doi/abs/10.1177/0265407512473006

Gaslighting

https://liveboldandbloom.com/02/relationships/emotional-manipulation

https://lonerwolf.com/gaslighting/

https://medium.com/@SoulGPS/getting-your-intuition-self-trust-back-online-after-narcissistic-abuse-a5d6247b4bda

https://medium.com/moments-of-passion/why-manipulative-people-manipulate-us-the-child-within-and-how-to-deal-with-them-2d5966c0c400

https://medium.com/the-mission/how-the-power-of-forgiveness-will-set-you-free-8b3c95068bc2

https://peaksrecovery.com/blog/effects-of-psychological-emotional-manipulation

https://positivepsychology.com/self-awareness-matters-how-you-can-be-more-self-aware/

https://psycnet.apa.org/record/1995-05356-001

https://slate.com/human-interest/2016/04/the-history-of-gaslighting-from-films-to-psychoanalysis-to-politics.html

Resources

https://themindsjournal.com/gaslighting-signs-psychologically-manipulating/

https://thriveworks.com/blog/gaslighting-techniques-manipulators-undermine-contradict-victims/

https://today.yougov.com/topics/health/articles-reports/2017/06/27/it-could-be-happening-you-3-4-us-adults-dont-know-

https://wehavekids.com/family-relationships/Musts-When-Coping-With-Scheming-Family-Membets

https://workplaceinsight.net/gaslighting-widespread-in-the-uk-workplace/

https://www.aconsciousrethink.com/6766/gaslighting-examples/

https://www.bestofthislife.com/2018/04/boost-self-esteem.html

https://www.businessinsider.in/The-9-terms-and-phrases-you-need-to-know-if-you-think-youre-being-manipulated/2-Object-constancy/slideshow/65718317.cms

https://www.bustle.com/p/7-signs-your-parents-are-gaslighting-you-42457

Gaslighting

https://www.entrepreneur.com/article/281874

https://www.goodtherapy.org/blog/psychpedia/gaslighting

https://www.goodtherapy.org/blog/psychpedia/silent-treatment

https://www.harleytherapy.co.uk/counselling/12-steps-to-overcoming-bitterness.htm

https://www.karen-keller.com/content/healthy-competition-vs-manipulation-how-tell-difference

https://www.learning-mind.com/attention-seeking-behavior/

https://www.learning-mind.com/gaslighting-techniques/

https://www.learning-mind.com/manipulation-techniques/
https://time.com/5411624/how-to-tell-if-being-manipulated/

https://www.linkedin.com/pulse/how-deal-sneaky-manipulative-people-dr-isaiah-hankel

https://www.nbcnews.com/better/health/what-gaslighting-how-do-you-know-if-it-s-happening-ncna890866

https://www.powerofpositivity.com/how-to-deal-with-a-manipulative-partner/

Resources

https://www.psychologytoday.com/ca/blog/communication-success/201805/12-failures-highly-manipulative-people

https://www.psychologytoday.com/intl/blog/communication-success/201406/how-spot-and-stop-manipulators

https://www.psychologytoday.com/intl/blog/liking-the-child-you-love/201707/5-ways-your-struggling-adult-child-may-be-manipulating-yo

https://www.psychologytoday.com/intl/blog/think-act-be/201811/when-is-it-gaslighting-and-when-is-it-not

https://www.psychologytoday.com/us/blog/enlightened-living/200805/understanding-constancy-in-relationship

https://www.psychologytoday.com/us/blog/here-there-and-everywhere/201701/11-warning-signs-gaslighting

https://www.psychologytoday.com/us/blog/in-flux/201610/9-classic-traits-manipulative-people

https://www.psychologytoday.com/us/blog/mind-in-the-machine/201808/trump-is-gaslighting-america-again-here-s-how-fight-it

Gaslighting

https://www.verywellfamily.com/is-someone-gaslighting-you-4147470

https://www.yourtango.com/experts/zita-fekete/6-most-commonplace-tools-used-manipulation

www.ingramcontent.com/pod-product-compliance
Lightning Source LLC
Chambersburg PA
CBHW020413080526
44584CB00014B/1312